SINGLETARY
ON
SINGLETARY

SINGLETARY —ON— SINGLETARY

Mike Singletary
with Jerry Jenkins

THOMAS NELSON PUBLISHERS
NASHVILLE

Published in Nashville, Tennessee, by Thomas Nelson, Inc.,
and distributed in Canada by Lawson Falle, Ltd., Cambridge,
Ontario.

Scripture quotations are from the NEW KING JAMES VER-
SION of the Bible. Copyright © 1979, 1980, 1982, Thomas Nelson, Inc., Publishers.

Library of Congress Cataloging-in-Publication Data

Singletary, Mike.
    Singletary on Singletary / Mike Singletary with Jerry Jen-
kins.
        p.   cm.
    ISBN 0-8407-7654-3
    1. Singletary, Mike. 2. Football players—United States—Bi-
ography. 3. Chicago Bears (Football team) I. Jenkins, Jerry.
II. Title.
GV939.S48A3   1991
796.332′092—dc20
[B]   91-24779
                                                            CIP
            Printed in the United States of America
    1   2   3   4   5   6   7   —   96   95   94   93   92   91

Contents

Contents

Part Six: On Thorny Issues

Acknowledgments

To the woman who has stood by me for better and for worse, who taught me how to forgive and love freely, and who continues to help mold me into the man God wants me to be. Thank you, Kim, for your love, support, and trust, and for sitting through those cold, rainy, unbearable days at Soldier Field—never missing a game, no matter what.

To my wonderful children who make our lives complete. May God continue to give us the wisdom and knowledge it takes to raise you to be God-fearing men and women.

To Mom, for being that example to a son you knew would listen and learn. You took the time to teach me and to show courage, standing strong when it would have been easy to give up. You held tight to God's hand, and He brought us through.

To Dad, the most persistent man I know. Thank you for never giving up. You kept trying to do the things that were right. Keep fighting the good fight. God knows your heart.

To my brothers and sisters. I love you dearly and don't see you nearly enough. Thanks for all your support. Let's keep praying for one another.

To my in-laws—mother, father, sister, and brother. If any man feels he has better, he'd better check out the competition.

To the Lord. Thank you for taking a boy who was going down and didn't even realize it and saving me, giving me a new heart, a new mind, and a new soul. Thank you for giving me your grace and a second chance. I didn't deserve it and still don't, but you keep letting me know that nothing I could ever do could keep you from loving me. Thank you most of all for sending your only begotten Son to die on the cross for someone like me.

And to you who have picked up this book. Remember that you matter to God. The proof is the cross of Calvary and the empty tomb.

Foreword

It was the evening before Good Friday. I sat in the back of our church auditorium watching our drama and music teams rehearse for the busiest and most exciting weekend of our year.

On the way back to my office I walked through our nursery area. While the "up front" people were busy in the auditorium, a whole army of behind-the-scenes workers were preparing for the chaotic influx of infants and toddlers the weekend would bring. Toys were being sanitized, linens folded, windows washed, rocking chairs dusted, and carpets cleaned. In one room a man with a familiar face and arms the size of tree trunks served quietly.

The Mike Singletary most people know glares ferociously across the line of scrimmage on prime time TV. The Mike Singletary I know humbly pushes a vacuum across a kid-stained carpet in a church nursery.

I have known Mike for ten years. I have been his teacher, his pastor, the officiant at his wedding, and his friend. As his teacher I have watched him lay a solid foundation for his Christian faith. As his pastor I have seen him live out his commitment to the local church by serving joyfully and giving of his resources liberally. As the one who married him and his bride, I have marveled at his devotion to home and family life; he obviously treasures his delightful wife, Kim, and he adores his children. As his friend, I have benefited from Mike's counsel and convictions. He has been a listening ear and a caring brother to me.

Television commentators key in on Mike's intensity. Those of us who know him well are inspired by his integrity. My life has been enriched by rubbing shoulders with Mike. Yours will be enriched by reading this book.

> Bill Hybels
> Senior Pastor
> Willow Creek Community Church
> South Barrington, Illinois

P.S. He's a pretty good middle linebacker too.

Introduction

Why This Book?

I've had a lot of offers from publishers to write another book since my autobiography, *Calling the Shots* (with Armen Keteyian, Contemporary Books, Chicago), came out five years ago. I enjoyed doing it, but I was very immature in my relationship with God at that time—though most people didn't know it. That's why it was good that that was mostly a football book.

I didn't want to do another football book yet. There are things I've wanted to say to young people and to parents, things with more substance than which Bear throws a chair through a wall or who's feuding with what coach. I'm a pretty quiet guy. I'm not going to force my opinions on people who don't ask. But give me a platform, ask me to tell you what I think, and you'll hear the straight stuff. If you keep turning the pages, I'm going to figure you're interested, that you're asking what I think about lots of things.

It might not be what you wanted to hear or what you thought you would hear, but it'll be honest. Frankly, I've said more in this book than I thought I would. I've admitted failure and been open about myself and my faults. But in talking about who I am, about being a real man, about achieving, and about what's wrong with this generation, I couldn't help but look at myself.

You're going to read some very disappointing things about me here, things I haven't said before, things I may later regret saying. But I'm committed to honesty. I ask only that you not use my failures as an excuse to fail yourself. Learn from them. Learn from me.

I know I'm a throwback to a simpler time. People tell me I was born too late, that I'm out of step with modern America. Well, you're going to find out that I wasn't always out of step enough. Yes, I believe in the old values, and I suppose I sound like an old man to some people. But maybe it's time somebody spoke up for the old-fashioned ways again.

Stick with me and see what you think.

Mike Singletary
Chicago, Illinois

SINGLETARY
— ON —
SINGLETARY

PART ONE

Singletary on Singletary

1

Who Am I?

I don't know how to talk about myself without sounding like I'm bragging. People who know me know I don't talk about myself much, but it seems like you have to know who I am and where I'm coming from before you're going to care about my opinions on life. To me, boasting is more than just talking about yourself without backing it up. Lots of braggarts *do* back up what they say, but they're still self-centered and obnoxious. I don't want to be that.

I'm what a lot of people call an overachiever. I'm at the top of my profession, and if you want the statistics and all that, you can find them somewhere in the back of this book. I don't like to emphasize all the stuff I've done in my career, but don't get me wrong: I'm very proud of it.

If there is value in talking about myself and my achievements, it can only be in the process, in how I've done it. Because, what I've done, anybody who sets his mind to it can do. Does that sound too easy? I'm not saying it's been easy. I'm saying that I bring to my job less natural ability and fewer physical attributes than just about anybody I know. So if I can do it in my profession, you can do it in yours.

Don't believe me? Picture an all-pro middle linebacker. What does he look like? Is he big? Is he fast? Is he strong? How big? How fast? How strong? No matter what picture is in your mind, it's not of me. The Bears are being generous when they list me at six feet tall. And I'm all but bouncing on that scale to make it hit the high two-twenties. I'm one of the two smallest linebackers on the Chicago Bear roster. Yet this year, if all goes well, I'll tie Walter Payton as the Bear with the most consecutive Pro Bowl appearances (nine).

So what's the process? How does a relatively small football player succeed on the field? I won't kid you and say it has nothing to do with the physical. I'm bigger, faster, and stronger than the average man. But on the field, where I'm facing linemen six inches taller and seventy-five pounds heavier, and where I'm trying to tackle running backs as big or bigger than I am, clearly my success has to do with the mind and the heart. I take full advantage of whatever physical gifts I have, and I work hard on building strength and quickness. But if there's one thing that sets me apart, it's attitude.

I'm not just talking about desire and dedication.

Lots of people have all of that you could ask for. And I'm not just talking about persistence, never-say-die, never give up, though that's a big part of it too.

I'm talking about something that includes all that and a lot more. I'm talking about obsession. People tell me they can see it in my eyes—the excitement, the intensity, the passion. How does obsession reveal itself?

> *I wished and hoped and prayed I would be bigger, but in the meantime, I was going to make the most of what I had.*

Through no short cuts. None. I take no shortcuts in life. There, I've said it. If it sounds like boasting, I'm sorry. But that's the secret to my success, and it works just as well off the field as on. People look at a guy like me, a kid from nowhere who has achieved what most boys in this country dream of, and they think I must be in a daze, shocked at my success. Oh, I'm thrilled. I'm excited. You'll find that I'm grateful for the opportunities I've had because I was born in America. But I have to tell you: The cars I drive, the house I live in, the things I have, my achievements are no surprise to me.

Somewhere along the line, a long time ago, I came to realize what would be required of me to excel. I wished and hoped and prayed I would be bigger, but in the meantime, I was going to make the most of what I had. I would not be denied. There would be no shortcuts, no half-stepping. You know what that is. Maybe you've done it yourself. To make it look to your P.E. teacher or your coach like you're going all out, you grimace and grunt and generate a lot of movement and sweat, but you're half-stepping. You're faking it. I see it all the time. Not only does it not fool anybody, but it also robs you of dividends. Take no shortcuts and do no half-stepping in your profession and imagine what you could do. The world would be at your feet.

Take no shortcuts and do no half-stepping in your profession and imagine what you could do.

I've learned the hard way that having the world at my feet is meaningless without being in a right relationship with God and my loved ones, but the principle remains. There is hardly anything a person cannot do who is obsessed with giving his all.

I have in my home a set of weight-training machines with gauges that count your repetitions. The problem—or the advantage, depending on your perspective—is that you can't fool the gauges. They won't give you that last rep unless you extend all the way. You can groan and pant and scream, but if you don't push or pull to a certain point, you don't get the rep. Anybody who works out knows that if you don't do the rep, you don't get the benefit.

I love those machines. I'll get guys in there with me and we'll be pushing each other, encouraging, badgering, whatever it takes to reach new levels of effort. The gauges are inflexible and unforgiving. I can just stand there staring at a gauge, telling my workout partner, "No rep yet."

"What?!"

"You haven't done it yet."

"No way!"

"No rep. Look at the gauge. You're not doing anything."

Talk about accountability.

Now here's what true obsession means: When I'm working out alone, I expect every bit as much from myself as I do when coaches or teammates or workout partners are watching. If I tell myself I'm going to get up at six in the morning and do a full workout, I get up at six, regardless. No shortcuts. No excuses. No exceptions. If I indulge myself and watch television till midnight or read until one A.M., that's too bad. I said I would be up at six; I get up at six. I said I would do a full workout; I do a full workout. I say I'm going to do twelve repetitions of something I've only been able to do ten of in the past, I do the twelve. I make the gauge record it. No cheating, no manipulating, no rationalizing.

I know nobody's watching. I know no one would ever know. But when that six-two, 235-pound fullback follows a pair of six-five, 265-pound guards into my zone, *I* want to know. I want to know I have done everything I needed to do to prepare myself. They're going to try to run through a six-foot, 228-pound middle linebacker, and I want to be the most primed middle linebacker they'll face. Within the rules and bounds of the game, I want to punish them, to make them regret wanting to take me on. I want them to learn why I have earned a reputation. I want them to know that I deserve whatever accolades or awards I get. Because of my size I had to be way better than average to even make it to the NFL. To excel here, I can allow no shortcuts, not even in private.

I want to be consistent. I want to be the same way in my personal life as I am on the field. In other words, will I be the same in private as in front of my wife? If a fine-looking woman strikes up a conversation with me, and it might seem fun and harmless to do a little verbal hitting on her, will I say the same things to her with my wife not there as I would if my wife *were* there?

I want to always be able to say that I did my best, and that I was just as committed to that in private as I was with people watching. It hasn't always been easy. It still isn't. But the rewards are worth it. A great evangelist once said, "True character is what a man does in the dark."

One of the ways I try to keep improving is to surround myself with people who will challenge me and make me better today than I was yesterday. Tough people. Not people who idolize me or agree with everything I say; that would be a dangerous thing to do. I wouldn't want to give the green light to criticize me to people who don't love me and have the right motives. It would be of little help to me if the people who were correcting me and reproaching me were jealous of me or mad at me. If they are truly concerned for me, I can take it. It still hurts; criticism is painful for anyone. But like those private workouts, facing criticism pays off.

So I try to keep in my life people who are smarter than I am, who have more wisdom, who have my best interests at heart, and especially people who love the

Lord. All of that is embodied in the most important person in my life, humanly speaking: my wife, Kim. I want her to correct me and suggest changes when she really feels it's necessary. I have feelings just like anyone, but in the long run, I appreciate her holding me accountable. I don't fear her and I don't consider her my God. But I want to be a better man, an improving man, and she is a major reason why I feel like I'm still growing.

I expect to be the best. If I don't go out there with that intention, it won't happen. The Lord has given me my gifts and talents, and the only way I'm going to glorify him is to do the best with those gifts that I can. Then I can say, "Here they are, Lord. Your reward. Your glory."

I don't get caught up in comparing myself with other people. I don't read the sports pages or listen to the sports talk shows. I don't have time for that. All I can do is the best I can do. I feel it's my responsibility to upgrade the linebacker position. I want to try to be better than Dick Butkus or Ray Nitchke or Jack Lambert, but not because I don't think they were great. They were great, great football players. But today we have advantages they didn't have in conditioning, training, and facilities. And the game has become so much more tactical. I want to carry on the tradition of those linebackers and raise the standard a notch for the guys coming up now.

I've had young linebackers, the ones on the smaller side, tell me that it was through watching me play that they began to believe they could make it, even though they weren't tall or massive. That makes me feel a little like Jackie Robinson or some other pioneer. I realize leading the way for down-sized linebackers is nothing like breaking the color barrier in baseball, but it makes me feel good anyway.

I have tremendous respect for those who have paid

the price in whatever area of life they're in. These are people who know what they're talking about. They're not telling me something because it's been passed on to them. They're telling me something because they've experienced it. They've been there.

That's why I respect Mike Ditka so much. He's been there. He's played. When he tells you something, you know it's true. When he tells me something, I can take it to the bank.

I used to have a hobby, when I had a little more time to myself. I would visit businessmen and pick their brains. One visit was with the flamboyant Texas millionaire, Ross Perot. In his office he had a sculpted eagle, and he explained to me that eagles never flock. I loved that thought.

When I got back to Chicago, I looked for a sculpted eagle for myself. I put an inscription on it: "Eagles Don't Flock." They live high on mountaintops. They have perfect vision. They do their own thing. If you're going to tangle with them, you'd better be ready. They know what they're doing, and they have tools most birds don't have. With their speed, vision, strength, and ability to fly, they are unconquerable.

That's how I want to see myself. I want to fly above all the junk down here. I won't cheat. I'll take the high road. I'll be a straight shooter. I'll take whatever chances are necessary to sell out for God.

It takes a lot of man to stand up for what is right and not to be afraid to be ridiculed for it. But if you choose to do that, know that people will also be watching you. I will get criticized for saying what I believe in (see next chapter), and I will also be held to my own strict standards. I will live with the ridicule, and I welcome the test.

A big word for a man who was born long after his time is *anachronism*. I admit it. That's me. I am an

It takes a lot of man to stand up for what is right and not to be afraid to be ridiculed for it.

anachronism. I would love to have been born in the 1920s or 1930s so I could have been an adult during the 1950s and 1960s. I'm a little too serious-minded for this day and age. Even my wife tells me that. She says I've got to loosen up a little. I try, but I don't see myself really changing. I like who I am and what I stand for.

I go to a modern, progressive church—Willow Creek Community Church in South Barrington, Illinois. They use drama and contemporary music, but Pastor Bill Hybels also preaches messages that are the most challenging I have ever heard. I grew up in a Pentecostal church, and while we were yelled at from the pulpit and made to feel like the lowest things on the planet, we were rarely challenged, rarely encouraged.

Even television has changed too much for my taste. When I was growing up, watching *Andy Griffith* and *Leave It to Beaver* and shows like that, we learned something. They were funny and entertaining. Maybe they were a bit dull and unrealistic, but they made points. They had morals, lessons, something to learn. When was the last time you saw a situation comedy that taught you anything but a new sexual innuendo? Even the kids on these shows are smart-alecky and sassy. Most of the double entendres come from them, and everybody thinks they're cute and hip.

I still try to find the old shows at odd times on cable. Call me a fuddy-duddy, but I love those programs. I also like westerns and old movies where heroes stood up to villains and believed in honor and truth and justice. Those are among the many things I believe in.

2

What I Believe In

I am a guy who is extremely proud of everything that he is. I am proud of being black. I'm proud of my heritage. My father's dad was German. His mother was black. My mother's father was full-blooded Cherokee. Her mother was half Mexican, half black. I'm a product of that wonderful mixture.

When I go back to Houston, to the Sunnyside neighborhood, my chest sticks out. This is where I was born. This is my street. This is my home. It's not what it used to be, and someday I want to help get the neighborhood back to the way it used to be, but still it is the center of my childhood memories.

I believe in work. I take tremendous pride in it. Whatever I do, I want to do it to the utmost. I believe I can never fail, as long as I try, and I'm not afraid to fail. I'm persistent. I got that from my dad. I'll jump in and say, let me try that. Bet I can do it. And if I fail, hey, I'll get it next time. If I want to do something and I put my mind to it, it's going to take an awful lot to stop me.

I believe in education. I think a person should strive to know everything he can, not only about himself, but also about the history of his country and of his heritage. About the Bible. About English, math, science, algebra, biology. You're limited only to those things to which you limit yourself.

> *You're limited only to those things to which you limit yourself.*

It's there, all the education you want and need, in libraries. I can pick up textbooks intended for high school kids and learn something. Just because I have a degree doesn't mean I'm smart. I can forget what I've learned. I believe in continuing to build upon what I know, continuing to read and ask questions—why, how, when, where—not being afraid to step out and be laughed at because of what I don't know.

That emphasis on education came from my mom, who wouldn't let me work while I was going to school. She believed I should put my time and energy into my studies. She was working three jobs, it seemed around the clock, and many were the nights I saw her crying because there was no relief. She still had kids to raise, no husband and father in the house, and no income from her children. We could have worked. We were willing. But she said we were helping out by learning and getting good grades. That was the contribution she wanted from us. What an example of hard work she was!

I believe in being honest and admitting your weaknesses and shortcomings. For instance, I have significant hearing loss in both ears and have since childhood. It could have been hereditary or it could have been from doing so much construction work with my dad and brothers when I was a kid. I never wore earplugs, even when I was running a jackhammer or using a sledgehammer. It's embarrassing to have to wear hearing aids, but if being willing to do that will help one kid be brave about his own handicap, it's worth it. Being embarrassed about it is nothing but pride, and I'm letting the Lord deal with me about that.

There has been one great advantage from my hearing problem. It has made me a good listener, something I have become proud of. When I'm talking with someone, I listen extremely well. I maintain eye contact and the speaker has my undivided attention. That helps me learn, and it also makes me a good friend. People like to be listened to.

By choice I have few close friends. It isn't that I don't like people; it's just that I believe in being more than a good friend. I want to be a great friend. I want to be the kind of friend I like to have. And that takes commitment.

What makes a good friend is not having to do things, not having to perform. With the five or six couples Kim and I feel real close to, I can call them up after three or four months of not seeing them and we pick up right where we left off. If we try to get together and can't make it, we don't feel bad or worry about grudges.

It's great when Kim is close to the wife and I'm close to the husband. That makes a double best friend. And if a friend ever calls me with a need, he's got it. My resources are his. If he needs me or something I can provide, all I need to know is when and where. And he's the same with me.

Kim and I really feel fortunate to have a few people we can call true friends. It's so easy sometimes to take friendship for granted. True friendship is hard to come by. I hesitate to name some one at the expense of others, but there is one couple that we really feel comfortable with. We can go with them anywhere and have a great time. We go on a trip with them every year, and we all look forward to it. We see eye to eye on most things, and we allow each other room for differences.

The husband and I enjoy just sitting and talking about life and deep things. A lot of guys would get bored with that, but not us. The last time we went to an island together it was cold and rainy. With another couple we might have gone crazy. We sat there for three days and just talked and played games and laughed all day long. When friendship survives a bad-weather vacation like that, you know it's real.

Ron, my best friend from childhood, comes up about once a year to stay with us for a week. We reminisce about the neighborhood and our families, and we're saddened by the news of guys our age who are in jail or dead. We remember the same music and enjoy listening to it.

Kim has a childhood friend who visits with her too, but there are only a few couples we both enjoy spending a lot of time with.

And I'm not a guy who always has his hand out, requiring help from his friends. If anything I don't let them help me enough. I'm independent and self-sufficient, so when I ask, I mean it. When a friend needs me, he becomes my top priority. That's the only way I know to be a true friend. True friends don't call and lay a guilt trip on you about how long it's been since they've seen you. That gets tiring. Friends are friends, now, next month, or even if I don't see them for a year.

It may sound strange to hear the tenth and last child in a broken home say he believes in family, but I do.

Friends should be like family. It may sound strange to hear the tenth and last child in a broken home say he believes in family, but I do. I believe that the family is the strength of this country. Nothing but God should come before the family in a person's life. If I have to give up something for the sake of the family, it's worth giving up.

The kind of family I dreamed about as a child was not the kind of a family I grew up in. In my mind I saw a great family as all the things that revolved around a positive, loving, caring group of people.

My daddy was a preacher. In fact, we called him Rev. But our family was in turmoil most of the time. My mother was advised to abort me. I had been a mistake. She was older when I was conceived, and the doctor predicted complications. Those complications came and I was a sickly child, the farthest thing from a potential pro football player you could imagine.

My parents stayed together because that tenth baby had come along, and it was twelve more years before they finally divorced. I had hoped for a long time that something would change, because I couldn't stand the tension and the fighting. It had to happen. It was a horrible situation to grow up in. A TV show from the 1970s had a line in its theme music that said, "Your dreams were your ticket out." That was me. My dreams kept me alive.

Though my father went on to another failed marriage, I still wish my parents would get back together and live happily married. Of course, that is something they would have to feel comfortable with. They live close and take care of each other like sister and brother, but many of us kids still mourn their divorce.

It seems the only time our whole family gets together is when something bad happens, like a funeral or a serious illness. Though we are spread far apart in age, I still dream of getting everyone together for a reunion. Most of them still live in Houston, so I may have to bus them all to the Chicago area to make it happen. Kim and I will have to organize a family reunion once and for all, whether down there or up here.

It's going to happen, and it's going to work better than the family businesses I've tried to start over the years. When I came into some money, I wanted to start a business that everybody in our family could be involved in. The only problem was that as soon as everybody started thinking about the family business, they had an idea of what it should be and how it should be run. Even though it would have been my money, they wanted to be executives, not workers. I mentioned a construction company, but I heard, "I've been doing that all my life." So, how about auto mechanics? "No, let's try the dry cleaning business." In the end nothing ever came of it, and that's sad.

Being the youngest, I didn't get to know my older brothers and sisters the way I wanted to. Now I want to make up for that. I want us to get together on a happy note and have a great time. No envy, no animosity, no nothing but fun and a good time so we can really get to know each other.

Kim comes from a wonderful, loving family. I want our own immediate family to be like that. We're trying to bring good qualities from each of our families to implement in our own home and children. We have created the Singletary Family Creed that our kids memorize as soon as they're old enough to talk. It consists of five rules that go like this:

1—Love Jesus.
2—Love one another.
3—Always obey Mommy and Daddy.
4—Always pray for one another.
5—Put family before friends.

The bottom line of my beliefs is the golden rule—doing to others as you would have them do to you. That has made me one who believes in speaking for people who can't speak for themselves, one who sticks up for the underdog. When I was in high school I seemed to gravitate toward the outcasts, the nerds. My friends were the people no one else wanted as friends. They were the short guys, the so-called ugly guys, the unwanted, the unathletic. I told them, "Hey, you're *my* friend. You hang with me. You eat lunch with me."

I was a popular guy, a good student, a football star. People wanted to be my friend. But I had a good memory for a childhood that was sickly. I had once been short and skinny and weak. I couldn't run and jump and play with the other kids till I was eight or nine, when my parents' prayers were answered and I began to grow stronger. I remembered being unable to join in the fun, being the outcast, watching from the sidelines. I don't ever want to forget that.

So when I saw kids who were looked down upon just because they wore their pants too high or had a bunch of pens in their pockets, I told them, "If anybody messes with you, let me know."

These were kids who blushed in the presence of girls, who were shy when anyone greeted them. But if somebody mistreated them, I'd speak up for them in a New York minute. I have never been able to stand it when people treat others unfairly, especially those who are younger or can't stick up for themselves.

Two guys in particular—I'll call them Al and Ben —were sharp academically. But they weren't cool enough for the in crowd. Just to make a point, when I was invited to a party, I always asked if Al and Ben were coming.

"No, man, we don't want them around. They're not cool."

"If you invite them," I'd say, "I'll think about coming."

"Man, we don't want to invite them!"

"Then I won't be there either."

The other kids already knew I wasn't into drugs or smoking or alcohol or women who thought it was cool to use profanity. I didn't even like guys who did too much of that, but I was—and am—old-fashioned enough to believe that a woman who uses profanity in public has no class.

There came a time on a drafting class trip where the cool dudes came by and took some of Ben's drafting tools. "Hey, these are nice!" they said. "We could use these!"

I didn't want a fight, but I wasn't going to let that rip-off happen. I was always careful not to be too loud or threatening, because that would cause, rather than end, a problem. "Ben," I said quietly, "do you need those?"

He shrugged.

"You want them back?"

He nodded. "Yeah, I really do."

I turned to the bullies. "Give them back to him. Don't do him like that."

That happened a lot. Nine times out of ten they'd give the stuff back. They didn't want to mess with me, but mostly I tried to make them feel small for picking on someone like Ben or Al. I don't know what it is about picking on a little guy that makes some men feel like big shots. Whenever I see that, I step in and defend the underdog, and I always will.

My dad learned a hard lesson about trying to solve things with your fists. He was jealous of a little guy who had made a pass at my mother, who was then Dad's girlfriend. Dad jumped him and the guy defended himself with a pencil. My father lost an eye. That was why he always told me to avoid foolishness and to pick my friends carefully. "Pick people who don't get into fights, because if they're your friend, you're going to get into those fights with them and mix it up to defend them. You'd better be sure they're worth it."

Even though my dad had a lot of shortcomings and wasn't always consistent in his Christian walk, he

My dad and my mother taught me my work ethic, the importance of listening and learning, to be a bottom-line person.

taught me a lot and I respect him and love him for that. My mother too. They taught me my work ethic, the importance of listening and learning, to be a bottom-line person. I'm not one who likes to deal in symptoms. I like to get to the root of a problem. If my wife is becoming critical of me, I try to decide whether I'm really doing anything differently than I've ever done it. I ask myself, *Why is that bothering her today?*

Usually I'll discover that her irritability with me is a symptom of something deeper. She may have a problem with me because of something I've said or done, or not said or done. I'm not saying that I can't be irritating, but she has learned to live with my idiosyncrasies just as I've learned to live with hers. So I try to cut to the heart of the problem. Rather than defend myself or argue the point, I'll say, "Honey, what's the problem? What did I do? What's wrong?"

She may not even realize until then that she's been critical or irritable, and even if she has realized it, she may not have been aware of why. But when I force the issue, it soon becomes clear what the problem really is. She tells me, I apologize, we talk it out, and we move on. Dealing with the bottom line is much better than messing with the symptoms. Man, I can really blow that sometimes.

I tend to be direct and to the point in my business dealings too, which puts people off a little until they get to know me. I'm not trying to be intimidating, but I'm not a small-talk kind of a guy. I want to know what is expected of me, what the deal is, and how I can best satisfy the wishes of my client. Athletes and other well-known personalities don't have the greatest reputations for following through on commitments, but I refuse to be lumped with that crowd. I am so determined to keep my word and be trustworthy that I am insulted if my motives are questioned. If you have a contract with me, written or oral, I will honor it. End of discussion.

3

The Public
Persona

One of the toughest things a person like me has to deal with is his own image. I know who I am, but all that most people know about me is what they see on television. They see this manic guy with the bulging eyes, looking hyper, smacking guys on the butt, and trying to get the defense coordinated. Then they see me trying to make or be in on every tackle possible. Our team has been successful, and I've been honored by a bunch of Pro Bowl selections, so I get interviewed a lot too.

I might seem a little soft-spoken compared to what people see in the game, but they find me—I hope—thoughtful and analytical. That's how I see myself. But that's it. That's all that people know about me. I don't care for them to know everything about me and my family and my private life, but what happens is that I become two people.

I am Mike, the real guy, the human being with emotions and a personality with quirks, strengths, weaknesses, likes, and dislikes. And then there is that other guy: Mike Singletary, the Bear, the linebacker, the visible personality. I try to be the same guy all the time, but sometimes people see what they want to see and hear what they want to hear. Sometimes I feel almost forced to play a role. When I go out in public, I am expected to be the Mike Singletary people know from their limited exposure to me on television. I cannot be the same Mike my wife and children know at home, much as I'd like to be and would feel most comfortable being.

It's not that I'm being phony. I'm just private, letting people deduce from that whatever they want. If I'm quiet and not smiling and they want to interpret that as my football persona, that's okay. The fact is that I'm still somewhat shy. I do have a hearing problem. I'm not a small talker. And I may be thinking ahead to my speech or some other responsibility. If my demeanor makes me look menacing, I'm sorry. It would not be me to paste on a phony grin and start slapping people on the back and shaking hands all around.

I have never had just one person represent me for all my outside engagements. I work with a few professionals on a project basis, and I've found that rewarding. For the most part, Kim and I handle my schedule. She helps me run the business of that public Mike Singletary. We get dozens of calls every few days for endorsements, autographs, speaking engagements, all of that. We even get calls from inventors with the latest training or football device who are convinced that if I could just see and try their gadget I would endorse it and we would get rich together.

We get calls from companies who have ideas and just want to bounce them off me. We get calls from others who have no ideas but want me to help them develop one. I would be crazy to complain about that. Such demand is what my work ethic on the field has afforded me. It has allowed me to make money off the field and to widen my ministry. I don't feel hassled by these people. Most of the calls are taken by Kim or our answering machine, and she and I can discuss things before I decide whether to even talk to the callers personally.

I get a lot of calls from churches. I almost hesitate to put this into print, but when I agree to accept an invitation to visit a church I do not charge an honorarium or expenses, unless it's out of state. The reason is simple. The gospel is not for sale. I'm just passing on the Word of God, which I hope everybody grabs. I can't charge for something I received free. I'm not in the business of ministry. I don't speak in churches to make money. I don't have a problem with those ballplayers who take an honorarium and give it to charity. But I don't charge churches.

If I set a reasonable fee, it would look exorbitant to most churches. Anyway, I go to churches for a larger purpose. I don't want the press there. I don't want photographers. I don't want parents standing in lines for autographs and pictures. What happens is that you wind up catering to the radio and TV people, talking football to the parents, signing autographs, and getting only about ten minutes with the kids you're really there to minister to. If I accept an invi-

*The gospel is not for sale.
I'm just passing on the
Word of God, which I hope
everybody grabs. I can't
charge for something
I received free.*

tation from a church, it's so that I can really serve the kids. Even then, I don't just greet them and sign for them and have a picture taken with them. I want to really work with them.

A church will have more success asking me to come and spend private time with a bunch of kids, working with them, teaching them, speaking to them, than they will asking me to help them raise money or get some public relations benefit out of my presence. When that happens, I'm just Mike Singletary the personality, not Mike the simple follower of Christ.

Now, after saying that, I must also say that I am very, very selective about those church invitations. Often people try to get around my polite "overbooked" regrets by calling without a set date. I know they're thinking that if they have set a date I can easily say I already have a commitment and get out of it that way. So they tell *me* to pick a date. I won't do it.

What I want is to hear the whole story of what

they're trying to do, what they have in mind, and how they think I can help. I want to know the date they're looking at. Then Kim and I will discuss it, decide whether it's something that will interfere with my top priority in this life—my family—and see if it fits the schedule.

The date is really not that important, because if everything but the date sounds legitimate and worthwhile, I may tell them that I can't make it then but would be open to another time. I don't want to be fooled. I would not like being asked to come and really minister to kids one-on-one in relative privacy and then find that all the adults showed up and the photographers and the press came to get a look at the football player. Telling me that you're sure my being there will draw a crowd is not the way to convince me. God is not into numbers. That's not something I want to be a part of. Some players like that kind of attention, I know. There was a time in my career when people would push me aside or ask me which one was Walter Payton, and I longed to be the one they wanted to see.

But as I get older (and hopefully wiser) and my priorities show a little more maturity, I see that being treated as a commodity is really not valuable to me or to the ones inviting me. I don't want to be rude, and I don't want to make up excuses about why I can't come. Sometimes everything will be just right, according to my requirements, and still I will simply feel that I should not go. Maybe I've done too many engagements or I have something else to prepare for, or I just want to spend more time at home.

The worst is when someone calls and says they've prayed about it and God told them I was the right person for the event. I have learned to tell them, "Well, until he tells *me* that, I'm going to have to decline."

I have also learned to say no without inventing reasons or even feeling the need to have them. A book on time management convicted me about being less than honest with people. It's hard to say no to thirty or so requests a day, and you find yourself being slightly misleading or making up excuses to make it easier on yourself. But that's nothing but lying, and I never want to do that. Kim or I now merely tell people politely that I am unable to honor their request and that we're sorry. Begging or making accusations of selfishness will not change our minds. Our decisions have been made through lots of interaction with each other and through prayer. All we can do is the best we can do based on that.

Some people can really be pushy. They'll say, "It's only an hour, and we'll come and get you." But if I've already decided it is not something I should do, all I can say is that I'm sorry, I just won't be able to. My spirit would not be right if I felt badgered into it. And if Kim and I have determined through prayer that it is not something I should do, I'd better not accept.

Now, for general speaking engagements, Kim and I decide on those in the same way, but of course that's part of my business. I'm there to be Mike Singletary, the Bear, but I like to be myself as much as possible too. Companies who ask me to endorse their products know full well what they're getting before we sign any deals. I will not endorse a product I'm not sold on, won't be associated with a company I don't believe in, and won't do anything silly or out of character.

I think these companies look to me to give them an image of credibility. I'd like to think I have a reputation for honesty and forthrightness, and I have no problem with a business arrangement where I can

I'd like to think I have a reputation for honesty and forthrightness

honestly lend that to a good company and product. The only time I run into problems is when a company questions my integrity or my commitment. They may have had problems with "stars" before, but I should not suffer because of the shortcomings of others.

One family-owned business I have had a relationship with wrote me a couple of letters while I was away from home on vacation for a month. We came home to hundreds of messages on the machine and hundreds of pieces of mail. One of the letters waiting for me the night we returned was from a new man at the business. It read, in essence, "I have written you twice and tried to call you four times without success. Apparently your relationship with our company doesn't mean as much to you as it used to, so perhaps we should get together and talk about our future."

In other words, if you want out of your contract, just let us know. That really bothered me. I couldn't wait to call him in the morning. I confess I was direct.

"Carl*," I began, "this is Mike Singletary."

"Hey, Mike! How ya doin'?"

I skipped the pleasantries. How did he expect me

* Not his real name.

to be doing after getting a letter like that? It was clear from his tone that he was trying to avoid the subject.

"Carl," I said, "you wrote me this letter, right?"

"Yeah, I—"

"Let me ask you this. Has there ever been a time when you've asked me to do something and I've said I would do it and yet I didn't do it?"

"No, but—"

"Has there ever been a time when I didn't return your call?"

"Well, I called—"

"Eventually. I mean, I've always eventually returned your calls, haven't I?"

"Well, yeah, but—"

"Has there ever been a time when I said I would be at a certain place at a certain time and I haven't been there?"

"No."

"No matter the weather or the traffic or my schedule, if I said I would be there, I was there, right?"

"Right."

"So why should I start lettin' you down now? I've been out of town for a month and I got back to hundreds of messages. All I ask is that because of my track record you give me the benefit of the doubt. Can you do that?"

"Yes, Mike. I'm sorry."

"I can understand your frustration at not hearing from me for so long, but why would you write me a letter like this?"

"Mike, to tell you the truth, I thought you might be trying to get out of the deal because you got a better offer and didn't know how to tell us."

"If you think that, you don't know me from Adam. That's not me. That's not how I operate. If I wanted out of the deal, I'd tell you straight up."

"I believe you would," he said.

"I don't do business that way anyway. I'm not even listening to other offers while our contract is in effect. My word is my bond and my signature is proof. If I say I'm going to do something, you can consider it done. We went on vacation because it was family time. If I can't go away for a while without getting a letter like this, maybe we *should* talk about the future of the relationship."

"No, no, no. I didn't mean that, Mike. I want us to continue."

"Okay," I said, "but we need an understanding, because this is no small thing to me. I don't want to make it more than it is, but if I agree to something, you can count on me for it, and it means everything to me that you understand that."

I hated to hammer the guy so hard, but his letter hurt. It had hit me right where I live: in my motives and intentions. It's hard work to live up to your obligations, and to have your heart questioned is too much. I think he got the message. He knows I'm with his company for the duration of the contract, and things have been smoother ever since.

I had a similar disagreement with a car dealership I've worked with for a long time. I overreacted to a problem and it was only my wife's good counsel that salvaged the situation. I believe strongly in being responsible for my own actions and mistakes, and she appealed to that in the end.

What had happened was this: My usual fee for a certain period of commercials and endorsements included a new car. When I was in the place to talk to the owner about the car, I saw one on the showroom floor that I really liked. I had not expected him to give me a car so loaded with options, but when I said how much I liked it, he had one of his salesman show me everything on it. If the owner had said, "I really hadn't planned to give you that much car," I would

— 33 —

have completely understood and either paid for the upgrades and options or been happy with whatever he was offering. But he agreed that the car I was looking at was equipped the same as the car I would receive.

Later when the dealership called to tell me my car had arrived, I drove out there to discover that the car they thought was mine was not the car I was expecting. "There must be some mistake," I said. "Let me talk to Doug*."

"He's on vacation, but this is the car he said to give you."

I showed them the car just like the one Doug said I could have, and one of them said, "Fine. We'll put those options on this one and it should be ready tomorrow."

The next day I called to see if it was ready. "Well, Mike, the thing is, we have to call Doug and make sure it's okay."

"Wait a minute," I said, still cool but getting frustrated, "make sure what's okay?"

"Well, to do what you said to do to the car."

"Listen, I didn't say to do it to the car. Doug already said it was okay and Ed* was standing right there when Doug said it."

"All right, um, Mike, Ed doesn't really have the authority to make that decision, so we're really going to have to talk to Doug."

"Okay, fine."

They talked to Doug by phone, he approved the work on the car, and they called me back to tell me. "It'll be ready tomorrow."

The next day I called and they told me they had a technical problem with the car. Something wasn't

* Not his real name.
* Not his real name.

balanced right, and they wanted to be sure it was perfect before they let me have it.

"Okay," I said. "I appreciate that. But we're going out of town for a week, so when we get back, I'll have my wife come and pick it up."

After we got back and Kim had headed out to the dealership, they called me. The car was ready, but Doug wanted to talk to me. Frankly I thought he might want to apologize for the mix-up. Nope.

"Mike, I can't do what you want," Doug said.

"Wait just a minute," I said. "Doug, we've been all through this. First you told me I could have that car, and then when there was a misunderstanding they checked back with you and you said to go ahead and give it to me. Ed heard you the first time, and your other guys got the word from you the second time. Now what's the problem? It's not like this car is a gift. It's payment for services, and if you wanted to just give me the basic car you should have said so."

"Well, Mike, you're asking for too much."

"Doug, I'm not asking for anything more than I asked for the day I was in there with you. You made a commitment. Do I have to get everything in writing from now on?"

"Well, maybe we do have to get everything in writing, Mike. I don't ask you to do that much."

"Wait a minute. Who are you talking to? We're supposed to be men here. We're supposed to be friends. We have a relationship. What is this?"

There was a pause. He could see I wasn't backing down, and of course I had a witness that he had promised me that car.

"I'll tell you what," he said, reluctantly, "I'll put everything on the car."

I said, "I don't want it on the car now. My wife should be there by now, and she's made a trip for nothing. Forget it. Just forget it."

"Mike, don't be that way. I'll make it right."

"No, Doug, you know what? I'm really glad this happened. I'm seeing you in another light, and I needed to see that."

"Mike, Mike. What are you going to do? Now we're just going to be mad at each other."

"No, I don't think I want the car at all."

I asked to speak to Kim and told her to just come home in the old car.

"No, Mike, he's getting the other car, the one with everything on it the way you wanted it."

"The way he promised it."

"Okay, but I really think you need to apologize."

"Apologize! Me? I'm not the one who forgot. I'm not the one who didn't keep his promise. I'm not the one who did anything wrong."

"Mike, listen. Whatever the situation is, you need to apologize."

"I'm not apologizing."

"You always talk about what a nice guy Doug is."

"Yeah, but look at what he did."

"Well, look at what you're doing."

"He was in the wrong."

"Yes, but you know better. As a Christian you've been given much, and much is expected."

"Well, I'm not apologizing."

I hung up and tried to busy myself with other work. I could think of nothing else. I thought, *You know what? As usual, she's right.* I headed toward the dealership. My car phone rang.

"What're you doing in the car?" Kim asked.

"I'm going to see Doug."

"Well, I'm on my way home in your new car. It's loaded."

"I told him not to load it up."

"Well, you're going to love it. It's nice."

When I got to the dealership, Doug was in his office. We looked at each other sheepishly, shook hands, and sat down. "Doug, look," I began, "I drove all the way over here for just one reason, and that's because I enjoy our relationship. If I made you sound like a liar, I apologize for that. But that car is not worth enough, the money you pay me is not worth enough to jeopardize this relationship. Those things just don't mean that much to me. If you want to take the car back and give me a basic car or no car at all, that'll be fine. I don't need that stuff. I have always looked out for you in this business, and you've always looked out for me. Let's continue to do that. I'm sorry."

"Mike, I'm sorry too. I talked to Ed and he remembered the original deal the same way you did. It was just a misunderstanding, and I apologize. We just heard things differently. I was saying one thing and meaning another, but Mike this is forgotten with me. I enjoy working with you more than anybody I've ever worked with."

"Well, Doug," I said, "you know I feel the same, because I get calls all the time asking me if I have a car deal. I don't even listen to their numbers, because even though they might be higher, I don't want to go with them. I want to stay with you."

"I know that, Mike. We take care of each other."

"Man," I said, "I didn't know what a stubborn old guy you were."

"I didn't know how stubborn you were either until today, Mike."

We laughed and re-established the relationship. He told me to enjoy the car, and I have. In the end, I was glad the whole thing had happened because it strengthened our friendship. I have to get things right. I can't let them go. They have to be settled. And my wife was correct. Right or wrong, it was my responsibility to reconcile. I'm glad I did.

I never want to quit working hard on interpersonal things off the football field. That's where the real challenges come.

I never want to quit working hard on interpersonal things off the football field. That's where the real challenges come. I mean, I love the game. It's my arena, my platform, where I'm the most comfortable. I want to talk about football and all that goes with it, but you need to know, as I've had to learn, that it's life off the field, life in the world, where the real differences are made. I've learned my toughest lessons in the nitty-gritty of everyday life. In fact, the biggest mistakes of my life have happened off the field. But let's talk some football first.

PART TWO

On the Football Business

4

In the Trenches

In many ways, football defines me. It requires hard work, preparation, thinking. Lots of things happen at once. The successful player has to overcome fatigue. The field is a place to perform, to excel. It's my arena, and I enjoy the privilege and the opportunity to play professionally more than I can say.

People make a big deal over how I look when I'm peering over the line of scrimmage into the opposing backfield. I wasn't aware of how I looked until I saw

*In many ways,
football defines me.
It requires hard work,
preparation, thinking.*

the pictures myself. Some guess that I look so bug-eyed because I'm not wearing my glasses, and I'm straining to see. Others think I'm trying to see everything at once. There might be something to that. Truthfully, I have no idea why I look like I do on the field. If I had to guess, I'd say I look so intense because I'm excited.

I'm excited because I'm prepared. Again, I don't mean to brag, but I doubt there is anyone in the NFL who watches as many game films as I do. And I don't just watch them. I watch them over and over and over. I'll stop and rewind and run a play in slow motion dozens of times, and I've been known to watch one play hundreds of times. You see, I'm trying to compensate for any lack of size with knowledge and preparation. I will study the opponent's offense so thoroughly that I will know what their options are by the way they set up.

I've had opposing coaches tell me after a game that they believe I know their offense better than most of their players do. I just might. They ask me if I've been reading their playbook. I tell them no. I didn't read the book. I saw the movie.

There are all kinds of plays an offense can execute,

and they are limited only by their formations. Once I see the formation and know the options, I look for the next indication of exactly which play is coming. Usually off of a particular formation you can run four or five different plays. Even narrowing it down to those is an advantage, but I want to know more. If a certain guy goes in motion, they're going to run the trap. If both receivers are on the same side before the snap, it's going to be a quick pass. If the receiver starts in motion and comes back, they're going to run a counter off tackle. If the receivers are split, they're going to throw to the tight end. The problem is, all those formations and their options are different for each team. Sixteen times during the regular season alone I have to sit and stare at the films of the opponent and memorize their offense. Someone told me once that if every defensive player in the league prepared the way I did, no one would ever gain any yardage.

Just like sitting in a college classroom and getting a test where you're sure you know the answers, I'm excited when I see the familiar. The hours and hours of lonely tape-watching pay off when I see the set up. My eyes grow wide as I watch for an end in motion or a quarterback licking his fingers or players switching positions during the count. My goal is to know by the time the ball is snapped exactly what play is being run and where the ball will go. I want to be the first one to the ball, to intercept it, to cause a fumble, to tackle the runner before he gains a yard. For me, football is anticipation. I see something, I anticipate the next move, and I'm ready. If I look excited, it's because I am.

I'm not saying there aren't a lot of guys who diligently prepare. Many of my teammates are big on watching films. Everybody has to do some of it. But I've yet to find someone who can stay with me all night watching game films. It's the price I'm willing to pay. I've always wanted to be the best at what I was doing. If I wasn't the best I wanted to find out how I could be the best. I'll do anything within the rules to accomplish that goal.

Staying within the rules is important to me. I believe in fair play.

Staying within the rules is important to me. I believe in fair play. If I have to cheat to win, I don't need the victory. I get frustrated with guys who cheat. I tell them. A guy who already looks twice my size holds me when I'm going after the ball carrier, and I'll say, "Man, is that the best you can do? I thought you were better than that."

They do it again, and I say, "Hey, I'm one of the smallest linebackers in the league. Why do you want to hold me?"

Some of them will say, "All right, I won't do that. You're right." Others say, "Well, if you'd slow down a little, I wouldn't have to hold you."

When my teammates and I watch the game film they always laugh when they see me get held. They say, "Look, now here's where Mike warns the guy for the first time."

They've been on the field with me, so they've heard what I say. They mimic me as the film rolls. I'm pointing at the blocker, saying, "Please don't hold me." The guys crack up. The second time they mimic me saying, "I told you once not to hold me, now I'm not going to tell you again."

"*Samurai*, man!" they say. "Why are you so polite?"

I'm not polite the third time. I get in the guy's face and I say, "Keep your hands off me now." If he gets irritated and tries to bump me, I bump him right back. Then somebody reminds me I'm a Christian and I walk back to the huddle. Then I have to pray for the guy instead of pop him. Which is the right thing to do but not as much fun. I have to say, most of the guys in the league are younger than I am, and they respect me when I try to correct them. If they don't, they respect me a few plays later. There's not a hold or a cheap move I haven't seen and don't know how to get through.

Holding is one thing. A cheap shot is another. That's dangerous. That could cost me my livelihood. If I get cut from behind, chip blocked, or crack backed, I'm on the guy right now. There are no warnings and no manners. I just tell him, "That will be the last time you do that to me." He's in my wallet when he threatens my health, and I can't tolerate that.

My image is of a thinker and a tactician. Most people would be amazed to hear me on the field. I've been called the thinking man's football player, but there's a lot of the dog in me too. I want to be a gentleman and lay the hammer softly, if that makes any sense. I don't want to overstate my case. But I love playing wild and I love screaming. The fans can't hear that in the stadium or on TV, but yes, I'm a screamer. I make noises on the field I never make off the field. I want the emotion as high as it can go. That's fun. That's the way I like it. Here comes the *samurai!*

That's the reputation I like on the field. Off the field I'd rather be known as a gentleman. A few years ago I was on the treadmill at the Cooper Clinic in Dallas when Dr. Cooper mentioned that Roger Staubach, the great Dallas Cowboy quarterback, "comes in here frequently."

That was interesting, because Staubach had been my childhood hero. Then Cooper said, "In fact, he's due in here today." Now I was excited.

A little while later Staubach came in and introduced himself. I was nearly speechless. He told me he appreciated the things I was doing as a football player, a family man, and a Christian. "I like what you stand for," he said. "You know, I've always told the Cowboys, you sure know how to pick 'em, don't you? They had the opportunity to get you in the first round, and they blew it big time. Anyway, I just wanted you to know how much I admire you and what you do."

"Hey," I said, "let me tell you the other side of the story. When I was a kid growing up in Houston, I watched you all the time. I watched you play, and I watched you in your interviews. Man, you were a player. Tough, smart, a gentleman, a fine Christian. You were everything I thought an athlete should be, so whatever I am today I owe in many ways to your example. You really helped a kid from Sunnyside."

That was a shock to him. He had no idea that he'd been my hero.

You might think that because I work so hard and prepare so much that I would be a coach's dream. Several of my coaches have said I was a "coach's player," but I have to say I don't always feel that way. There *is* another side to me. I *will* speak my mind. I always try

to speak in love and not to embarrass anybody in authority, and I won't do or say something just because
I think I have the power to do it. Sooner or later that
power is not going to be there, and people remember
when you took advantage.

But there are times when I feel it's necessary to go
to a coach and talk to him in private. Mike Ditka and
I have had some great talks, some not so great. Some
people say they wouldn't want to play for a guy as
fiery and crazy as Ditka. I can't think of anyone I'd
rather play for. He hates losing as much as he likes
winning. He's intense and obsessed, and I resonate
with that.

If I think he has said something or done something
wrong, I'll tell him. I usually begin by saying, "You
may think I'm one of the dumbest or most arrogant
players you've ever seen, but to be honest with you, I
don't care. I'm after the same thing you're after, and
that's to win. To win we have to play together and
play for you. If you really care about that and about
this team, consider this." And then I'll tell him that
maybe something he tried isn't working, or that what
he said to a guy hurt him rather than helped him. I
might say he was wrong to criticize the defense for
something.

I always finish by saying, "I know you don't report
to me. I'm not your boss. I'm not expecting you to
tell me what you're going to do about it. Just think
about it, will you?" And then I leave.

Of course, I never do that unless I'm convinced I'm
right. No head coach wants a player, no matter how
long he's been in the league or what his reputation is,
correcting him or lecturing him. I don't see it as that.
I see it as trying to work together and being honest.
Nine times out of ten, I see a difference within the
next few days.

One of the reasons I like Ditka is that he's a

straight shooter. He was a hard-nosed player, and he knows how to get on people. There have been times when he's been upset with me. He'll blame me for the defense breaking down or not appearing prepared. I'll usually say, "Coach, wait a minute. Settle down. You can scream and yell and throw stuff or do whatever you want, but I'm not leaving. I'm not going anywhere, because I've got to talk to you."

"You're supposed to have these guys ready!" he'll tell me. "Why weren't they prepared? The middle linebacker on defense is like the quarterback on offense. He has to be a leader. Being a good player is not enough. You have to take charge. Good players don't win. Good players who are leaders win. To be a great linebacker, you've got to be a great leader."

"What do you want me to do?" I ask him.

He'll tell me he wants me to light a fire under somebody. Challenge him. Get him to play with more intensity. "When I played, I told guys that if they didn't start carryin' their weight around here, I was gonna knock their blocks off. You've got to do that."

"All right, coach. All right. I'll talk to him. If that's what you expect of me, I'll do my best to get it done."

Sometimes I ask him where he sees me as a player. He hates when I do that. "Maybe the best linebacker ever," he says. "Don't know yet."

"Where am I right now?" I ask him.

"Well, when was the last time you really put a hit on somebody?"

"Last week."

"Really? When was the last time you broke your helmet?"

"Well, it's been a while."

"I want to hear one break. I want to see one."

I look for criticism from the toughest critics on the team. My good friend Shaun Gayle is one of the hardest guys to please. I'll make twenty tackles in a game and ask him what he thought, and he'll say, "Mike, I expect that of you, man. What do you want me to say, it was great? It was good. Good job."

> "Mike, I expect that of you, man. What do you want me to say, it was great? It was good. Good job."

Dog, man! Is that all I get?
That keeps me psyched. After all these years and all these hits, everybody wants to see that one good pop each game.

5

For the Fun of It

I enjoy getting to the play and surprising people with my speed, which is better now than it's been for years. Not a lot of people know that I had arthroscopic surgery after the 1988 season. Though I started well in '89, I was unable to do enough weight training during the season to bring the knee back to full strength. That seventeen-minute operation took over a year to heal. In the off-season I was able to run hills and do all the other things I needed to, so now I'm like a kid in a candy store. The speed and strength is back, and I feel reborn physically. I don't want to make any rash predictions, but if people thought I looked better last year, this year, Lord willing, will be more than interesting. And that's an understatement. I'm going to be ready.

I take onto the field an attitude that says, You come through me, you're going to pay. *That's what makes it fun.*

I take onto the field an attitude that says, *You come through me, you're going to pay.* That's what makes it fun. I'm not trying to hurt anybody, and I feel terrible when I do. But within the rules, I'm going to give a guy a pop to remember when he comes through the middle. My favorite, most exciting play is the one that comes right at me. I can take that all day.

I respect every player I come across. I don't care what his reputation is, good or bad. To have made the NFL, he has to have ability. No matter what he looks like on film, I'll prepare for him the same way I prepare for everybody. For every guy who makes it, there are hundreds sitting at home watching on TV who think they should have.

I know that after all my years in the league, the

guys on the other team's offense know about me. Whatever they thought I was or heard I was or think I am now, I don't want to disappoint them. When you're a linebacker, your game is nailing the ball carrier. On defense you seldom get the opportunity for a solo tackle, so when it's just you and the ball carrier, you want to make the most of it. It's worth all the film you've watched to be there a step ahead of the ball, when you're an unpleasant surprise to the offense.

When you see a linebacker get to the ball a step late, he takes as much punishment as the ball carrier. He may have a lot to do with the tackle, but he's hit as much as he hits, takes as much as he gives, and it's not as much fun. The key to avoiding that is to get that repetition in your mind from the film all week. Then, when you see the play coming on the field, you have to convince yourself that you're right. Anticipate and get there.

What can mess up the mind of a guy like me who studies film so much is when someone says, "That guy is not predictable. He won't go for the old moves. He's too smart for that. What we did last time against him won't work this time. He's looking at the films too."

But all I can do is believe what I see. My mind is in motion and my will follows my mind. It's like taking a test. You see those questions and you know the answers and you're grateful you studied. I see that other team get into a certain formation, I watch for the trigger that tells me which play it is, and I have to put out of my mind that they have been watching the films too. Unless they've invented something new since the last game I watched, here comes the play I knew was coming. I may think, *I can't believe they're doing it again*, but the opportunity is there. The hole is there for just a split second. If I'm already moving,

I can be there before the ball. That's when good things happen on defense. If I guess wrong, I'm on the hot seat when we watch the films. Coaches have a way of making you squirm.

Though I respect the guys I play against, nobody intimidates me. In fact, the bigger they are and the stronger and faster they are, the more I enjoy the challenge. I'm out there to be the best and to win, so my attitude is: Bring it on! Give me your best guys and let's go at it. I try to make them regret coming at me, but a lot of them have the same attitude I do. They like the challenge too, so instead of turning tail and going somewhere else the next time, they want another shot at me. That makes for good football. They keep coming and I've got to keep bringing it.

When I get a chance to land a clean hard shot on somebody, it's scary and exciting at the same time. You're so primed, so pumped, so prepared that you really let a guy have it and you want to shout, "Yeah!" But then you look at the guy to be sure he's okay, and if he doesn't get up, you feel like a jerk. The first thing I want to know is that they're okay. Those guys have wives and children and mortgages and car payments just like I do. There might be some satisfaction in hitting a guy who's never been hit that hard before, or in breaking my helmet on someone else's, and there is even a certain sense of a job done well when a guy is slow in getting up or has to sit out a play or two to clear his head. But no way am I looking to hurt anybody. I just want them to know they're in a game and that Mike Singletary is on the other side.

In 1988 I hit Sylvester Stamps in Tampa Bay, got him clean but good and hard. Vinnie Testaverde had let him come across the middle and dumped a short pass to him. Man, I ran right through him from the side, really whopped him. He went down and didn't get up. Someone asked him if he was all right, and his eyes got big and his tongue stuck out. The trainer came out and said his pupils had dilated. I prayed for him. I could have easily defended myself and said I was only doing my job, that it was legal. That was true, but it wasn't what I was thinking just then. I cared about him and his family, his career, his obligations. I mean, we're out there to have fun, not to get crippled. The last thing I would ever want to do is ruin a guy's career.

He missed the rest of that game, but he came back fine after that. I was glad. I didn't lighten up on the next play, but I sure thought about it. You start doing that in this league, though, and you're finished. They'll eat your lunch.

I'm not one to celebrate big hits. Guys going crazy over every sack and tackle is something that's come into the game since I came into the league. I also think it's cheap to stand there and point at a guy you've just leveled. You see guys all the time pointing and shouting and rubbing it in. That's tacky, and those things have a way of evening out. I think it's okay to congratulate each other when you've made a good play, and I've been known to scream with excitement when everything goes right. But you won't see me strutting, dancing, pointing, or sticking my face in the ball carrier's face and crowing about it.

Someday they're going to figure out a way to put a tiny microphone in the players' helmets and the fans are going to hear what's really going on out there. Already on some films you can hear the grunts and groans and big hits. I wouldn't want anybody to hear how crazy I sound with my screams and noises, but those guys who try to show up the other team are really going to be embarrassed.

Just before the play starts I'm barking at everybody about what I think is coming and what they should do. If the quarterback audibles, I change the call. If he audibles again, I change again until he's out of options. I love it. It's the best job in America. I always thought that at some point I would start thinking, *Just another year or two and I'm done with this.* I've even said stuff like that, but I didn't really feel it. It sometimes seems like it's time to move on, but the game is changing. The competition is much bigger and the strategy more complex than when I came into the league, so I have to keep training and learning. That's what I love, so until my body betrays me —and believe me I'll know before it shows—I'm making no final decisions. This year I'll be a player/coach, maybe the only one in the league.

I like to meet people on their level. People who hear me on television interviews or in speeches know that I am fairly articulate and know proper grammar. But when I'm talking to people who are comfortable with street dialect, or if I run into old friends who want to talk the way we did as kids, I can slip into that easily. I'm not so concerned about precision then. Communication is what counts, not sounding uppity or condescending. If they get down to just plain ignorance, I have no time for that. And I'm not going to gossip. If somebody gets into that, "Did you hear about so-and-so and what he did?" I cut him right off at the pass. I'll say, "Hey, man, if I was in his situation I don't know if I might have done the same thing." Then I try to say something positive about the guy. That pops the gossip's balloon.

I know there are times when guys think I am too self-righteous. For some reason they quit talking to me or start avoiding me. I never let that get out of hand. I know how important it is for a team to stay together and be harmonious. Usually, I'll seek a guy out and ask him if there's something bothering him, if I've offended him, or anything like that. Sometimes he'll tell me there's nothing wrong and I can tell there really is. I'll think, *So, that's how it's going to be, huh? Maybe next time I won't talk to him.* Nine times out of ten I'll find out that he's forgotten about whatever it was, and here I am continuing a little disagreement that either never existed, faded away, or wasn't worth worrying about.

If I can tell a guy is really having a problem with me, though, I'll confront him in a minute. I want to get things straight. I don't like tension in the air, and I'm happy to admit it and get it right if I've done or said something that bothered him. It's hard for me to play with a guy I feel has a problem with me.

I might say, "Hey, the others say when I spoke to you it seemed like you were a little cold, or like you had something on your mind you wanted to tell me."

And he may say, "Well, you know, Mike, as a matter of fact, I did. I didn't like the way you spoke to the rookie who was trying to get the play right. I thought you were too hard on him."

And I might say, "Really? Well, maybe you're right. But you know I've been pretty patient with him, encouraging him and all that, but he's still a step late on that play. When I got a little tough with him he responded and made the play."

"Yeah, but now you got to let him know you noticed so he'll feel good about himself again."

"Maybe you're right," I'll say. "I'll talk to him. Now are we okay? I'm sorry if I lost your respect."

Other times guys will just deny they have a problem with me, often because they don't and I'm just being overly sensitive. I try to read people, and I think I can usually tell when something's wrong. But sometimes I'm mistaken. Even then, my trying to keep things right between me and my teammates helps those relationships.

The reason I try to be sensitive is because I know it's hard for big, tough football players to admit their feelings have been hurt. They think they're not sup-

---

I know it's hard for big, tough football players to admit their feelings have been hurt.

---

posed to do that. They've been macho, banger-type guys all their lives, so nothing's supposed to reach them. But I know they can be hurt because I'm easily hurt myself. If I have a disagreement or argument with somebody, and at the end there's still tension, that bothers me. I want it settled.

That even happens between me and the coaches. Sometimes, in the heat of battle, I'll call a defensive play that conflicts with what the coach wants. I know better; we've talked about it, but at the time it seems like the right thing to do. No matter how it works out —sometimes things work and sometimes they backfire—I usually hear about it when I get to the sidelines. The coach will say, "Mike, don't do that!"

I'll respond angrily, "All right!"

The next day I'll feel bad until I go to that coach and apologize. "I was wrong," I'll say. "I'm sorry about that. I was just trying to do what I thought was best for the team at that point."

More often than not the coach will squint and seem
to be racking his brain to remember what I'm talking
about. And when he does remember, he'll say, "I've
already put that out of my mind. Don't worry about
it."

But I do worry about it. I'll tell him, "I know
you've forgotten about it, but I haven't, and I want
you to know that I know my place. I'm the player and
I want to do what you say."

A lot of times the coach won't even know what
incident I'm talking about. It's not very often that we
players apologize for anything anyway.

If another player has said or done something that
really bothers me, they know I'll come right at them.
If it's a big lineman, like Dan Hampton or Steve Mc-
Michael or somebody like that, he knows I wouldn't
dream of trying to intimidate him, so I can be a little
stronger with my approach. I might say, "I want you
to know I didn't appreciate what you said yesterday,
and I think you're a sorry rascal for saying it."

If it's a rookie or a running back, someone younger
or smaller than I am, I take a little different approach.
I know I already have their attention just because I'm
a veteran, so I don't have to shock them by calling
them rascals or anything. I'll just say, "I don't think
you handled that right yesterday. I didn't understand
what you were trying to do. Would you explain it to
me?" That opens the way to real conversation.

If I'm the one who has caused the problem, I usually know why. Sometimes I don't and they have to
tell me. But like most people, I know when I've
crossed the line. I may be working on a certain move
during practice and I'm so immersed in it I forget
we're going three-quarter speed and I'll really pop a
guy. I may not think about it until I can tell from his
body language or his stare that I've been too aggres-
sive. I get that straight right way.

I start thinking, *Dog, that wasn't right. I would get fired up if a guy did that to me.* I'll go to him and say, "Hey, what I did back there, I'm sorry. I apologize. I wasn't trying to hurt you. I just slipped and gave you more than I thought. It didn't make sense to hit you that hard."

Usually they're so shocked they shake it off and move on. It's so important to me to keep all the relationships on the team right, because I am one of only five guys on the Bears with ten or more years of experience. The others look to us for how to act and react. They take their cues from us on how to feel about management.

The longer you're on a team and the more you contribute, of course, the higher your salary goes. You still want to be accepted by your teammates, but when you start getting called a superstar, everybody looks at you differently. All of a sudden you're the management's guy. After all, management has committed a lot of money to you. And the other guys don't want to be around you so much anymore. That could be a real problem if you weren't prepared to deal with it.

6

Management's
Guy

Nobody wants to be called management's guy, but it's what you get called when you've been around a while and start making the big dollars. There's envy. You become part of the establishment. You're talked about. Somebody is always bound to say, "Well, I'm better than that guy. I'm bigger, quicker, stronger. They just want to give him the money." You always get bickering from the gossips on a team.

A lot of guys can't deal with it. In fact, most guys

can't. The only way I've been able to is to not see myself as a superstar. I don't demand special privileges. I don't strut my stuff. I try not to be aloof. I'm quiet anyway, so I have to work at making sure I talk to everybody, show openness, show a willingness to listen and to talk. I know that one of the prices I pay

---

I want to be gone before people start saying, "Singletary used to be the best, but now so-and-so has passed him.

---

for wanting to be the best at my position is that if I reach that goal, I have to accept all the pressure that goes with it. I want to be gone before people start saying, "Singletary used to be the best, but now so-and-so has passed him. He's younger, quicker, and all that." Once you've reached the top, the pressure comes to stay there and to not fall. The pressure of getting there is much easier to take.

One way I keep from seeing myself as a star is to remind myself that everything I have and am is by the grace of God. No matter what I do, everything I achieve will one day be forgotten. Two or three years after I retire, it will be Mike Who? Oh, there will be those who mention me in the same breath with Dick

Butkus. He's still remembered by experts and long-time Bear fans. But the new fan, the new kid growing up puts the names Butkus and Sayers and Wade and even Halas in the same category. Someday the name Singletary will be part of the Bear past, and there will be those who won't remember what position I played or whether I ever made the Pro Bowl, let alone for how many consecutive years.

They can build up the next guy as big as they want. They'll say he's quicker than Mike, maybe better than Mike. I'll be asked what I think, and I'll be honest. If the next Bear middle linebacker looks better than I ever was, I'll have to say so. I'll also say that I wish they had taught him in college or somewhere along the line how to deal with the pressure. No one will ever tell him what it's like. He'll go from realizing his dream of being a professional football player to becoming a starter, then a standout, then a Pro Bowler. Then he may become a name, mentioned with the greats. He'll be recognized everywhere he goes. He'll be in demand to speak, to endorse, to sign. He'll make more money than he ever thought possible, and unless he has good counsel or principles to start with, he'll do the wrong things with it.

The worst part will come when he starts believing his press. When he hears his predecessor say, "Yes, he may be the best ever." Then, if he's not prepared, he'll be in real trouble. He may never have the staying power or the good fortune physically to stay around for ten years or more and really make a name for himself. He may believe his press to the point where he forgets the hard work and dedication that got him where he is. If he starts thinking he is a born middle linebacker who doesn't have to work out the year around and that he can stay on top even though he's not in the shape he was once in, it will all start to crumble for him. I've seen it happen to players on both sides of the ball.

Every once in a while you'll hear about some innovative university prof who has decided to have a course for budding professional athletes. He'll show them a contract, tell them about agents and percentages and the pressure of fame. The problem is that only someone who has lived through it can really teach it. Unless you've been through it, you can't tell anybody about the pressure, about the fear, about the emptiness of being at the top when all you're living for is yourself.

It can be empty, lonely, and scary at the top. And only a certain few can be at the top on each team. There will be a top one or two in the offense backfield, maybe one on the line. There'll be a standout or two on defense. You'll see these guys hanging out together. They have something in common. Special team players run together. Second stringers become friends. First round draft choices are a special breed. Guys find their niches, find out what they have in common, and form cliques. Yes, it even happens in the NFL.

There are very few stars who can really lead a team. Very few. For instance, if a guy is at the top, if he's seen as the best in his field, and he wants to tell the team something, he is sometimes suspect. He may make a speech, asking the guys to do something together as a team. But some may say, "No way. I'm not doing that. I've got more to lose than management's guy does. He's not going to be hurt like I am. No matter what he tells me, I'm not going to do that."

But if they know this guy is not going to sell out, if they know he's a real person, they'll follow him anywhere. They will watch, however, to make sure he never dogs it in practice, to make sure he's hitting as hard as he ever did.

What too few of the young players realize is that the better and bigger the deals become for the established players, the better and bigger the deals will become for everybody. I have been guilty myself of looking around the league and being upset that other players at my position are making more than I am, when I believe I do a better job. I have used that in negotiations, but it doesn't pay to be bitter or envious. If some rookie lands some gigantic contract that pays him more before he's even played a minute of pro ball than the ten-year veterans get, it only bodes well for the rest of us. A new standard has been set, a new mark against which everyone can negotiate. And don't think all these agents don't know what everyone is making. I don't even use an agent for negotiations anymore, and I have a pretty good handle on the salaries around the league.

Negotiating a contract can be as fun and challenging as playing the game. It's a game in itself, and it takes a lot of internal fortitude to stay with it. It can also be very discouraging. The same people who want to keep you pumped and motivated to do your best on the field are now trying to devalue your worth so they can justify paying you less. They tell you you're part of a family, and we love you, and we want to do all we can for you without hurting the other members of the family.

Most players wouldn't dream of trying to negotiate their own deals. They don't have the guts to sit there, eye-to-eye and toe-to-toe with corporate giants. They don't have the courage to refuse an offer or ignore an emotional plea that doesn't make sense. They would buckle under the pressure of being called unreasonable or selfish, and they would panic over missing something in the fine print.

*Most players wouldn't dream
of trying to negotiate
their own deals. But I
studied business in college.*

But I studied business in college. I knew I would
one day have to manage my own funds, and I didn't
want a certain percentage of it taken right off the top
because I depended on others to represent me. I can
read. I care. I study the marketplace. I know my
worth. And I enjoy the challenge. I can be stubborn,
and I've had some strained relationships over the
years, but in the end I've been pleased with what has
come from my negotiating.

The first time I dealt with the Bears, I used a friend
to try to get me the best deal he could. One of his
parents was Korean and the other American, which I
would not have dreamed would have become an issue, but it did. Jim Bob went in to talk with Jim
Finks, who was handling player contracts for the
Bears back then (he's now with the New Orleans
Saints and was a leading candidate to replace Pete
Rozelle as football commissioner before Paul Tag-
liabue got the job).

I was a second round draft pick in 1981, but I
wanted first round money. I knew I would succeed
and be valuable to the Bears, whether they recognized it or not. So I told Jim Bob what I wanted,

wished him the best, and waited to hear from him. The first call I got was a frantic one.

"Finks looked up from his newspaper and asked me what I wanted," Jim Bob said. "I told him I was there representing Mike Singletary, and he threw me out. He said I wasn't even an American!"

I covered the phone and cracked up. Of course, Jim Finks was just feeling him out and playing with his mind. Finks has proven to be one of the classiest guys in the league. Jim Bob wasn't mature enough to know that intimidation was just a tactic all executives use. When I got back on I tried to pump up Jim Bob. "You're the man! I'm counting on you. You're representing me, so you just march in there and demand to negotiate."

Jim Bob gave Finks the figure I was after, and Finks somehow ran him off again, so I decided to lie low. The Bears knew my number, and if they wanted me, they were going to have to come after me. I was working out in Houston when Finks showed up near the Bayou where I was running the hill. He found me and introduced himself. I was pleasant but unsmiling. I had not appreciated how he had treated my representative, taking advantage of his inexperience.

"Hey, we've got to get this straight, baby," he said. "You're going to be a Bear and we both know it, so let's come to terms on something that will be acceptable to both of us."

"You know what is acceptable to me," I said, not unkindly.

"Hey, we saw you play. There's no sense haggling. Let me show you some other second round contracts so you can see how fair we're being. You can tell me what you think."

"I can tell you what I think without looking at the other contracts because I don't see myself as a second round pick. I'm not your second round guy. If I come to camp I'm going to do things no other linebacker can do. I can't come in and play the kind of football I can play for the Bears for what you're offering me. When you see me in camp, you'll realize that. I think what I'm asking is pretty cheap."

I wasn't trying to be a big shot. I just believed in my heart that they had me underrated, and I think that ten years later they would agree. Finks was still playing hardball. He said maybe they would work something out later, hinting that by then I would have lost my chance to find a place on the team. "Maybe mid-season," he said. I knew I was supposed to be scared and see my chance at the NFL going up in smoke.

"I'll be right here," I said.

A week later he called and we made a deal. I didn't get all I wanted, but I got a lot more than what they were offering at first. Every few years I would negotiate another multi-year deal, and while I believe in honoring your contracts, it has never stopped me from trying to re-negotiate little things. Sometimes I've been successful. Other times I've been told, "No, we just went through all this last year. Live with it!" And so I do.

In the mid-1980s we had a particularly bad time and I didn't think I was going to return to the Bears. My pride was hurt. I felt underpaid. I wasn't being ridiculous. I wasn't asking for considerably more than anyone at my level. It got to the point where Kim had to step in and help get the thing right. It worked out well. The next negotiation went very smoothly. I wanted to be among the highest paid linebackers in the game, because I was considered among the best. We settled at a base I was comfortable with, plus a lot of incentives. I was happy.

We've since negotiated a new contract and I'm now paid among the top two or three linebackers in the league. I know a lot of people argue that no one needs the kind of money we make and that a Christian certainly shouldn't demand or expect it. I'm not listening. When it comes to my contract, I know what's fair. I see what's happening in the league. Sure it sounds crazy for grown men playing kids' games to make more money than the President of the United States or more than doctors, lawyers, and educators. I'm not going to say that we have to make it while we can, just because we have so few years to make it, because most people wouldn't make what the stars make in twenty-five years on their jobs.

The fact is, the sport is profitable because it's popular, because it is connected to television and advertising, and because it is played at a high level. If there is big money in the game, it only makes sense that a significant portion of it go to the players who make the sport what it is. If the sport wasn't generating that kind of money, nobody would be making it.

I've sat in the front office and been told, "Mike, this is really hurting us. We've made you a good and generous offer. We're trying to be fair and equitable, and this is all we can do."

Once I was talking to Bears president Michael McCaskey. He took the we're-trying-to-do-the-right-thing-for-everybody approach, look at the big picture, the whole perspective, which I understand. I listened. It wasn't that his points were not valid. It's just that the offer was not acceptable and what he was saying wasn't justifying it.

I was due a significant improvement in my deal, and when he shoved it across the desk—after telling me how hard they'd worked on something fair—to be honest, I was disappointed. I said, "What do you think I am? What do I look like to you?"

He gave a double take and said nothing.

"I try hard not to be stupid," I said. "I do my homework. I know where I fit in this league, and this offer is well below that. When you think we can get together and talk about something that's fair to the team and to me, let's talk again."

Now you have to understand, I'm not that hard of a guy to get along with. I'm not belligerent, and I try to never be inappropriate. I wasn't being disrespectful toward Mr. McCaskey, just toward the offer. I was insulted, and in my heart I would not have been able to play with that on my mind.

"Mike," Mr. McCaskey said, "wait a minute. What is it you want? What's the problem?"

I turned. "I want to be respected," I said. "I want to be treated with some dignity. Don't treat me like I don't know what's going on or as if I haven't become one of the best players in the league at my position, that's all."

After that I dealt with Ted Phillips, director of finance, who handles all contract negotiations now. Usually when they get to the point of asking you what you want, you're getting somewhere. But sometimes it's just another game. They ask you, you tell them honestly, and they say, "There's no way we can get close to that." Then you start all over again.

It happens everywhere, in every front office in every sport. They tell you they love you and that you're family, and then you hear of guys getting traded without being informed in advance. It's a business. We all know it's a business. It's fun and it's exciting and, yes, probably all of us would do it for nothing if we had to. But we have to fight for our positions and our deals because we're in business too. When we become too expensive to justify, when we're not good for business, we're gone. We know that and we accept that. So while we're good for business, the business has to be good to us too.

Negotiations require a lot of prayer, because neither Kim nor I want to see me do or say something rash. Because I am sensitive and emotional, it can be a painful time when I feel I'm being treated unfairly. I just try to keep focused on what I need to do. I prepare as diligently as I would for a game, and when I go in there to negotiate, I don't want to be treated like only a player. At that time I am an executive too.

At some point I am going to leave the game on some terms. I'm going to be hurt or old or for some reason unable to contribute as I should. Somehow,

---

It might sound strange for someone who calls himself a Christian to be so concerned about money. The point isn't money. The point is justice.

---

it's going to happen. So while I'm there and healthy, I want only my due. I don't want to be crazy about it or ask for something out of step. I just want to be fair and to be treated the same. I want to be a gentleman and be treated like one.

What it comes down to, in the end, is who am I really playing for? Who do I represent? Supremely, Jesus Christ. It might sound strange for someone who calls himself a Christian to be so concerned about money. The point isn't money. The point is justice. I believe God would have me be as thorough and diligent in negotiations as he would have me be as a player or as a husband and father. I would be no testimony to anyone if I let myself be treated unfairly simply because I was unprepared.

I try to remind myself where I came from. I am the boy from Sunnyside. I represent a family. I represent my parents, my brothers and sisters, my teammates, the fans. I focus on that whole spectrum when I play, and I always give my all. I know I'm in an entertain-

I know I'm in an entertainment business, but I don't look at it that way. To me it's an opportunity to give back to God what he's given me.

ment business, but I don't look at it that way. To me it's an opportunity to give back to God what he's given me.

And it's fun. It's grueling and painful and sometimes seems hardly worth the effort, but don't let anyone tell you it isn't fun. That's why we play. The only time it's not fun is at cutting time when that rookie roster gets cut down to size and some of the veterans are told they won't play another down as a Bear. That's hard.

You've sat with a kid and had him tell you that he has a dream, the same dream you had, maybe of getting his mom a house. Of doing things for his brothers and sisters. Of being a great player one day. And then he gets handed that pink slip. All you can do is look him in the eye, knowing how much it hurts, and hurt for him. Occasionally one of those decisions is a mistake and the cut player goes on to another team and does well. But, usually, he is done. And all you can say to him is, "Hey, man, best of luck to you. May God be with you. I'll be praying for you."

PART THREE

On True Forgiveness and Reconciliation

7

The Painful Time

When I first started dating Kim, neither of our families were thrilled. Her people didn't know me and my people didn't know her, but both sides were convinced it wouldn't work. My mother was offended that her family would question whether I was right for her, and some of my sisters felt I was insulting black women by dating a white. Kim's family feared she was just being rebellious for the first time or marrying me only because I was a football player. I believe they were truly more worried about the pressures on the children of a mixed-race marriage than they were about the fact that I was black; we were concerned about the same thing.

I knew almost from the beginning that I had met the woman God had for me. Kim was pure. What you saw was what you got. She was honest and straightforward with no deceit and as vulnerable and transparent as she could be. She was a girl willing to try things. She was not a wimp, not a quitter. I had the feeling that if I married her and things got tough, she would hang in there with me. I knew if I fell on my face, she would be there to pick me up and encourage me and keep me in the game.

We were out driving one time, and I was so convinced that she was the woman for me that I stopped the car and said I wouldn't drive an inch further until I knew she was willing to marry me. She said I could drive on.

That's when I started asking her hundreds of questions. What if this? What if that? Her answers were dead on every time. What if I run out of money? She'd say, "Then we'd be out of money." What if the Lord sends me to Africa to be a missionary? "Then we'd go to Africa." What if I have to go back to Houston and take care of my mom or dad? "Then that's where we'd go." What if you get tired of my family, the different culture, and all that? "It'll never happen."

And it hasn't. When I took her down to meet my family, Kim immediately went to the kitchen and began cooking with my mother. They hit it off from the beginning.

What if I have to go here? What if I have to go there? Kim would say, "I'll be your wife, you'll be my husband; I'll want to be with you. Your people will be my people and your God my God."

I didn't worry about people who said we would be

unequally yoked. We were both Americans. We were both Christians. We were both human beings. Most of all, we were both in love. We believed God wanted us together, but I worried about whether her family would come around. She had been a model daughter and, if the truth be known, they would have advised against this marriage.

But Kim never wavered. Her position was, she was going to be with me. If that meant getting ousted from the family, that would be their loss. She never actually came out and said that, and I think she knew her parents would eventually accept me. She was a pillar of strength to me. I was afraid because I wanted our children to know and love *all* their grandparents. I had a lot of things going on in my life and in my head, but when I saw the strength she exemplified, I realized, oh man, she really does care. She loves me and wants to be with me.

My questions continued. What about the future? "We'll be together." What about your parents? "It's going to work." What about my family? "I'll become part of your family."

She was good as gold, as real as they come. She didn't pull any punches. I found we could go anywhere and be with anybody and she could deal with them. I didn't know what people thought or said, I just knew I wasn't going to spend the rest of my years wondering what my life would have been like without Kim. She was the love of my life, and true love is not easy to find. Even after you find it, it is only a seed that can die if it isn't nurtured. Losing Kim was not a risk I was willing to take. I accepted that there would always be some who wouldn't understand that our love crossed the boundaries of color.

We got married in May of 1984, and almost immediately Kim knew something was wrong. The man who had put his best foot forward during the courtship was now a sullen, moody, self-centered man who wanted his own way. When she was critical or disagreed with me, I clammed up and wouldn't talk to her for a day or two. When I was in a decent mood she tried to find out what had been wrong with me. I wasn't talking. I was confused, guilty, and troubled, and she had no clue.

We had been married at Willow Creek Community Church in South Barrington, Illinois. Kim, believing we were both solid believers, wanted to attend the church on the weekends and on Wednesday nights. I had all kinds of excuses not to go. I saw myself becoming like my own father. Distant. Quiet. Sullen. Angry. I didn't want to be like that. I tried to pray, but nothing was happening. Something in my life kept me up at night and made me miserable and irritable during the day.

Willow Creek is a modern church that really knows how to appeal to the unchurched. There is drama and contemporary music, and they make people feel welcome and comfortable without putting them on the spot. It was a wonderful place, but I found fault. I didn't want to be there, so nothing was right about it.

I told Kim the church was too big. I grew up in a church with fewer than fifty people. Willow Creek drew thousands. It was too much of a show, I said. The music wasn't my style. They sing too much. I don't hear enough of the Word. That was a laugh. It was the Word I was trying to stay away from. That mirror to my soul made me look away, turn away, stay away.

Kim was devastated. She would ask me, "Mike, why are you acting like this?"

I told her I didn't know, that I needed to be alone, to think. I needed time. I needed space. She knew

It was the Word I was trying to stay away from. That mirror to my soul made me look away, turn away, stay away.

before I did that what I really needed was to forgive my dad. We were in Houston visiting, and he would come by. I was cordial, but then I would ignore him. I was partial to my mother. Kim would tell me, "Mike, that's not right. He's still your father, no matter what he did. He doesn't seem that bad."

"You weren't there when we were growing up," I'd tell her, "when he would just up and leave for long periods. You weren't there when he was preaching on Sunday and being unfaithful to my mom during the week. You weren't there when he left her and left us and took up with another woman."

Kim and I continued to talk about it when I wasn't too angry to respond correctly. Finally the day came when I realized that I had to do something about my feelings toward my father or I would never be free to grow. I called him from our home in Highland Park one summer day in 1984, and we had a two-and-a-half-hour conversation.

I told him the truth. I told him I was angry at him, that I felt hatred and bitterness toward him for the kind of a man he had been. I told him he had been hypocritical to preach the gospel and live the way he did. I told him he had abandoned my mother and us kids, and that marrying someone else broke my mom's heart.

We did some yelling and screaming and crying, and he learned that I knew things he thought I'd been too young to remember. When I got it all out, he tried to set me straight. "I want you to know something," he said. "One of these days you're going to find out it's not as easy as you think, being a father. And not all the fault was mine either. I'm sorry for the things I've done, and I'm sorry for not being the kind of father you wanted and needed. But I don't owe you any apologies. I kept a roof over your head and food on your table. I tried to do the best I knew how, and that's all I really knew to do.

"There are a lot of things you don't know about me and our situation, and there were a lot of things I wouldn't have known to teach you or give you. How could I be expected to be a better father when I didn't even know how?"

I grew up a lot that day and for the first time in my life, I realized that you can only give that which you have received, whether it be happiness, hatred, love, or grace. All my life, my dad had seemed like a loser one minute and great the next. That's just the way he was. As a family man and as a husband, he was pretty much a failure. On the other hand, when you got him outside the house as a worker, he could do anything. He strove to teach us kids a good work ethic.

His childhood was tough; his mother died at 38. His father had a job in the city and the family lived in the country. His father came home on weekends. My dad was the oldest kid at home then and had to pick up the job of mom to his younger brothers and sisters, in addition to attending school. This went on for about six months.

When he felt his younger siblings could care for themselves, he left to live with his mother's sister in San Antonio. He lived with several uncles and aunts until he ended up in Hendersonville, Texas, where he met my mother.

During that time, he continued school, until he reached the eighth grade. Moving from town to town and having to work too, he couldn't keep up with regular classes. He had to drop out of school. But even after he dropped out, he didn't stop his education. He continues to pursue knowledge, to this day, in any way he can.

Mom's recollections of the early years of their marriage are pleasant. Dad read the Word of God every day and they were happy. The first few kids did well. But when the pressures came and more children arrived, he wasn't able to handle it.

When I was little it seemed Dad was always gone to a church meeting or to bid on a job. It's amazing to me that the marriage lasted as long as it did. I believe they loved each other, but with Dad's inconsistencies and Mom's not knowing how to hold a marriage together, as life went on it became tougher and tougher to survive the wounding of each other.

If I make it sound like my dad was sometimes good and sometimes bad, that's the way it was. I didn't have a lot of father-son talks with him. He would tell me if I was going to do something to do it right and to take some pride in myself and my work, but there wasn't much dialogue back then. Now we really had a chance to talk.

The conversation got cooler and I began to appreciate my dad. I could feel the bitterness melting away. I knew he could tell I was forgiving him as we talked. "Things just happened, son. What can I say?"

Once we got through it, I loved him with a new love. It was unbelievable. Ever since then, when I see him we hug and kiss and I tell him I love him. And I really do. I enjoy him so much. We talk and have a great time with each other now.

But all was still not right in my world. God used that forgiveness and reconciliation to start a real work in my heart. I felt free to try to be the kind of man I knew God wanted me to be. But when he turned the spotlight on me, I didn't like what I saw. I told him I didn't want to be a father and a husband like my dad had been, and the Lord told me to look inside myself. It wasn't pretty.

I felt free to try to be the kind of man I knew God wanted me to be. But when he turned the spotlight on me, I didn't like what I saw. I told him I didn't want to be a father and a husband like my dad had been, and the Lord told me to look inside myself. It wasn't pretty.

Twice, on trips out of town, I found myself in situations I shouldn't have been in. I would never and could never be unfaithful to my wife, but I was playing with fire. I was allowing myself to step over lines that would have crushed me if my wife had done the same. I called Kim and told her how much I loved her. "What's wrong, Mike?" she asked.

"I just wanted you to know how much I loved you," I said. Memories flooded back of how I had treated her during our engagement, things I had never told her, things that tormented me now. What could I do? I was miserable. Kim was in anguish, seeing that something was clearly wrong but unable to penetrate my angry wall.

Eventually I realized that I was under attack. Satan was after me and my marriage. He wanted to take me out, to ruin something that God had put together. I prayed, "Lord, don't let me get into trouble. I can't do this. I don't want to do this. I know what I want. I want Kim. I know the kind of a family I want."

At home I would lie awake in bed, night after night, sweating, staring at the ceiling. I was in misery, and for the first time in my life I truly believed I was about to die. When I could stand it no more I would get up and pace or sit alone in a room. I couldn't stand to be in darkness. It scared me. Kim worried, and I know she was praying for me. She wanted to know what was wrong. I pretended not to know, but I knew all too well. I just wasn't prepared to talk to her about it yet. I hoped I would never have to. I hoped it would pass, this guilt, this feeling that I had to own up to the fact that I was not what she thought I was.

She thought she had married a vibrant, deep, Christian, a man who didn't just talk about his faith but also lived it. I talked a lot about God and his work in my life. I said I was grateful for everything he had given me. I played the part well.

When I was able to sleep I began having bad dreams. That was no way to live. Sleeping that way gave me no rest. I was guilty during the day and tormented in the night. I was not a pleasant person to live with. God was dealing with me in a deep, personal way. I could run from church. I could make excuses why I didn't want to go there often. But I couldn't run from God. As much as I wished and hoped the guilt would go away in time, it wasn't happening. Every day it was worse. I thought I was going crazy. I knew I should talk to Kim, but I didn't want to hurt her. And I didn't want to face the truth about myself. I was not what she thought I was. Not even close. I had sold her a bill of goods and never delivered. How could I ever explain that or make up for it?

I realized I had a choice. I could continue to live a lie, live with deceit, and live with guilt. I could make a lot of money from my profession, acquire a lot of possessions, buy my wife clothes and jewelry and anything else she might like. I could have children, dress them nice, send them to good schools, and watch them grow without imparting any wisdom. I could have everything this life had to offer except peace and a clear conscience.

Or I could face myself and my sin. I could come clean with my wife the way I had dealt with the hatred and bitterness and unforgiveness I felt for my father. Only this would be much harder. Confession would start me through a long dark tunnel with the light at the end. Somehow I knew if I could ever muster the courage to do it, God would hold my hand in the darkness. And if by being honest with my wife, I lost her, he would still be there. I was not disowned by my father for telling him my deepest feelings about how I felt he had abandoned the family, but if I had been, God would still have been there.

I knew it would be the hardest thing I ever did in my life, but after a while I realized I had no choice. I could not have chosen to continue harboring my guilt and my rage even if I had wanted to. It was eating me alive. It was no way to exist. My loving wife was a constant stab of painful guilt to my soul. She loved me and cared about me and took care of me, but she didn't really know me. I knew she was loving a man who didn't exist. Mike Singletary, the man of God, was a sham.

I knew she was loving a man who didn't exist. Mike Singletary, the man of God, was a sham.

The only time I had any reprieve from the guilt was during practices and games. I took out my feelings on the field, and I became a ferocious, focused player like never before. But when practice was over or the game had ended, I had to face it. Every time I thought of it my stomach tightened and my head throbbed. I had been married just a few months, but it seemed as if I had been under this pressure for years.

I had been sullen, distant, and demanding since before we were married. She sacrificed a lot for the relationship. I was a guy who had to have time alone, time to think, time to write in my journal, time to pray, time to ponder. At least that's what I told her. If she complained about it, I told her that going with me was her choice. She could choose otherwise any time. If something wasn't good for me, it didn't happen. Everything revolved around me. She saw my potential and some of my deeper qualities and figured I was worth the risk. Now, a few months into the marriage, she had to be wondering.

I had considered myself a Christian, but there was so much inside me that prevented me from being used of God. I asked the Lord why I couldn't accomplish anything for him, why I didn't have control in some areas of my life. It was almost as if he spoke aloud to me. He said, "You've got to get that pride and sin out of your life. Then I can use you."

That hurt. I knew he was right; but, like anyone, I wanted the easy way out. I wanted my sin to just go away. I said, "Lord, let this just be between me and you. I confessed it. Let that be enough." But it didn't work that way. My sin had affected more people than just me. I realized that starting with me, inside me, would be difficult. But I had to start somewhere.

Even during the process of thinking how to go about it, how to tell my wife about the real me, I felt no peace. Sometimes when you plan to do the right thing, you feel better about life and never get around to doing it. That was not going to work in this case. I had to plan it, set up the right—or at least the most convenient—circumstances, and get my confession in the open.

If anything, my thought processes became more confused at that point. I had a sense that I was planning what had to be done, but the more I visualized myself actually breaking the news to her, the more dreadful it sounded. How could I do that? How could I disappoint her? How could I risk losing her?

God kept working on me. There was no question he wanted to get started. I knew that the result would be peace for me, a great relief at getting something off my chest and my shoulders. But it would be at Kim's expense! I would be relieving myself of guilt and causing her deep pain. Was it worth it? There was no easy answer. I knew I couldn't go on much longer bearing the burden of guilt. But it wasn't fair to dump on her.

On the other hand, it wasn't fair that she should be living with and married to a man who was only a faint image of his real self. She was living a lie too, only it was a lie I had created. She was married to and in love with a false impression.

I knew the secret lay in obedience. There had to be peace in that. Even if the unspeakable happened and she lost all faith and trust in me, lost her love for me, was so disappointed that she had to leave me, I would have to be content that I had been obedient. It would hurt me to hurt her, but the alternative was to keep it bottled inside me. I could no longer do that.

I wouldn't beg her to stay. I wouldn't challenge her if she just couldn't live with the man she would dis-cover me to be. I would rest in the knowledge that I had done what God wanted me to do, and that he would eventually be her support too, whatever hap-pened to us. I didn't like the thought of being apart from her, but if that would be one of the prices I would have to pay for finally doing the right thing, I would have to live with it.

8

My Confession

I booked us on a flight to a Caribbean island for a week. There were only huts. No phones. No TVs. Not even any air conditioning. Kim was encouraged, I think. She thought we were going to get some time away, alone together, away from the busyness of our lives. We had been married just a few months, and before summer training camp we were going to get reacquainted. That's what she thought.

I knew there would be little vacation. I knew that

not long after we got down there, I was going to come clean and tell her what I should have told her months before. I had tried. There were times when I had steeled myself and then was unable to force the words from my mouth. I hadn't had the heart to do it, and that was more true than I even knew myself.

But with the phone call to my dad had come a new freedom in my spirit that would have been wonderful if it hadn't been for what else God's light had showed me there. I could not become the husband and father I wanted to be the way I was. I knew if we could be away from home, alone together in the middle of no-where with no distractions, I could confess.

That didn't make the trip any easier. I'm sure my mounting tension showed. And I'm just as sure that Kim was hoping I would be able to relax and sleep better in the tropics. Maybe I would lighten up and loosen up and be more like the guy she thought she had married. I gave her a couple of days of peace and relaxation. The place was beautiful and the weather and sand and sea were great, but I couldn't enjoy them.

Finally the day came when I could put it off no longer. I told her I needed to talk to her. She must have thought that sounded strange. I mean, there we were, only the two of us in our little hut on the beach. I had to keep reminding myself that I was do-ing what God wanted me to do. I had to be obedient. There was no way out of hurting her, and maybe that wasn't fair, but it couldn't be avoided. I didn't want to use her for my own redemption, but she deserved the truth and the chance to start over. The choice would be hers; I would be obedient regardless. I was fully prepared for the possibility that I might be com-ing back from that trip alone.

We sat across from each other in the room.

I was fully prepared for the possibility that I might be coming back from that trip alone.

"There's something I've got to tell you," I said, my heart banging. I could see in her eyes that she knew something important was coming.

"What is it, Mike?"

I hesitated. There would be no stopping now. I just had to phrase it right, to get it out so it could be dealt with. I didn't want to beat around the bush and start by telling her how much I loved her and all that. This was a confession. I was going to lay it out and let the chips fall.

I took a deep breath and sighed. "All the time when we were dating, when you thought I was being true to you, I wasn't."

I had said it. She stared at me, her eyes filling. Mine were too. "You mean—?" she said.

I nodded. "All those times I said I needed to go think or do something else . . ."

"You were with other girls?"

I nodded miserably.

"You mean you—?"

I nodded again and apologized for the first of hundreds of times for the rest of that week. I assured her that I had never been unfaithful to her after we had been married, though I had found myself in a couple of situations a married man should never have been in. That may have been of some comfort to her, but not enough. I saw her spirit disintegrate before my eyes. I had cut her deeply, as I knew I would, and I felt worse for her than I had ever felt for myself.

"You deserve to know that I was not the man you thought I was, Kim, and I'm so sorry." I asked her if she remembered a certain time when I had said I was going a certain place. She did. "I was seeing someone else."

"We were engaged then, Mike," she said, crying openly now.

All I could do was nod in shame. I asked her if she'd rather I not give her any details. She wanted them all. She wanted to know who, when, and where. The only thing I couldn't tell her was why. With every detail she seemed to die more in front of me. I felt a strange peace, but that only made me feel guiltier. Some of the guilt of my sin was leaving with the confession, but the burden of what I was now doing to her weighed heavy on me. I knew I was being obedient, and I knew if we survived this we would have something special. But who knew what would come of it?

I wanted to touch her, to embrace her, to hold her and tell her how much I loved her and how sorry I was. But the time was not right. I saw the respect she had once held for me float away with her tears. I saw her trust fade and her pain build. All I could do was to repeat that I was sorry and that God had showed me my sin. I told her I was starting over and that I would be the man God wanted me to be from then on. I couldn't change the past and I couldn't take away the pain.

She would ask about other times and other people, as if taking it all in one dose would make it go down easier. The problem was, I didn't remember every-thing. And as I remembered it, I would feel com-pelled to tell her. I always asked her if she'd rather not hear it, but she insisted. I felt as if I had plunged a knife into her and that with every added detail I pushed it deeper and twisted it. The more I told her the worse I felt and the more she died.

Needless to say there was no more vacation after that. That little hut became her torture chamber and the fresh breezes and beautiful sky and sea were wasted on us. It was hard to look her in the eye the rest of the week.

Kim was more than hurt. She was angry. She felt betrayed, lied to. Which was true. She also felt dumb. "I was a fool for trusting you," she said. How could I argue? I knew even my apologies sounded empty now. My pledges of a new trustworthiness sounded hollow to her.

All I could say was, "Whatever you feel toward me, whatever you feel like doing or saying, feel free. When you're finished, I'm going to be right here."

I didn't expect immediate forgiveness. I was in de-spair. I was the one person who could help her through a blow like this, but I was the one who had caused it too. I'm sure she didn't know how to feel or even what she thought about me or our future just then. Like me, she had taken a huge step of faith to enter into what anyone would agree was a high-risk marriage. She had stood firm against all opposition. She had bolstered me when I had my doubts and fears. She had believed in me and loved me and cared about me and encouraged me. She was there for me, assuming I was all of that for her too.

And now this. I had been a phony. I had been a liar. A cheat. Irresponsible. Unfaithful. I was embar-rassed to be near her. I had humiliated myself as much as her. What more could I say or do? She owed me nothing, and I would have predicted nothing.

That night as we lay in bed together, not touching, not sleeping, I sensed movement. I looked at her in the faint light and saw her shoulders heaving as she wept. I deserved that punishment. She didn't. She deserved nothing but the best God had to offer her. I wanted to be that. I had failed so miserably.

I was in a vicious cycle. She was suffering from my sin, but because I had confessed she was feeling worse than I was. All that served was to make me feel worse. I tried to channel that remorse into a life-changing pledge. I would be everything God wanted me to be for the rest of my life. I knew that the only value in me was because of his work and the death of Jesus Christ for my sins.

Only he could produce any-thing good in me, but he expected fruit from my life. Discipline would be required.

Only he could produce anything good in me, but he expected fruit from my life. Discipline would be required. I could take the same determination I took to the football field and apply it to my daily life. I would get into the Scriptures every day and find out what the truth of God really was. I was tired of all the old platitudes about positive thinking and God helping those who help themselves. I had heard people say that we take one step and God takes two, and all that. It sounds good, but I haven't found it in the Bible yet.

I wanted to start keeping a journal from my prayer life and from the Bible that was more than just what I thought about things of life. If Kim could ever see her way to believe in me again, if she could forgive me and work with me to start over, we could have a marriage to be proud of. I knew I didn't deserve a second chance, but I hadn't deserved salvation either.

I knew I didn't deserve a second chance, but I hadn't deserved salvation either.

With every movement of the bed, every sob I heard, every tear that coursed down my own face, I renewed my resolve. How could I have done this to the one person I loved more than anyone else on earth? I prayed and prayed that she would survive this wound and that we could move on from here.

She would stop crying, roll over, and ask me another question. I'd tell her the ugly truth, and she would slowly turn away from me to cry again. I can only imagine her pain. I can't imagine mine being deeper. If I could have been the target instead of the cause, I might have been able to bear it better.

I didn't want her to leave me but I knew she had every right. I believed that if she did, we would get back together if our love was true. I was convinced that our love could overcome even this, but I knew it was a lot to ask. With each passing day, as we looked forward to heading back home, I was more encouraged. She still could have gotten back to Chicago and packed up and left, but she said nothing about that kind of a plan. You can imagine how sheepish I felt in front of her. Everything I did for her looked as if it was motivated by guilt and shame.

Even though it wouldn't have made any sense, because of my ego I could have begun to resent being the guilty one. I could have told her I had borne enough and that she now just had to forgive me. I could have said I didn't want to hear any more about it. That might have been true, but it sure didn't seem the right thing to say then. I told her instead, "You can ask me any question any time, anything you feel like asking, and I'll tell you the truth. If I was going to lie, I wouldn't have told you all that. If there's something not clear, just ask, and I'll tell you everything."

She took me up on it. The next several weeks were the most painful in our marriage.

Mike Singletary. Hard work and dedication to excellence have paid off in his ten seasons with the Chicago Bears.

Mike is known as "Samurai" for his wild screams and jarring tackles.

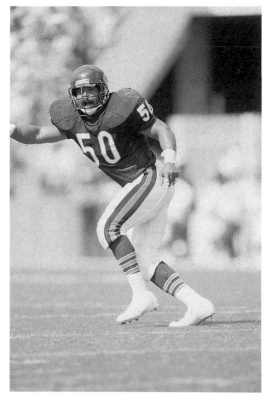

No short cuts and no half-stepping have made Mike one of the best middle linebackers in history. He confers with fellow linebacker Wilber Marshall during a play against the New England Patriots.

Opposing coaches accuse Mike (here against the Cincinnati Bengals) of knowing their offense as well as their own players do.

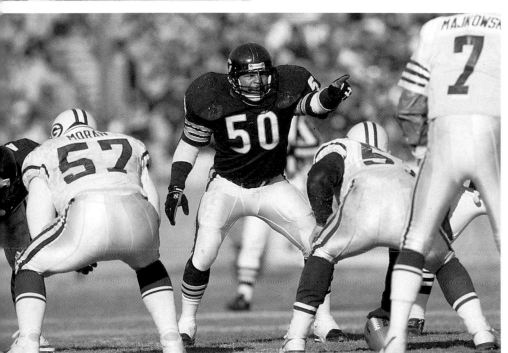

As captain of the defense, Mike memorizes the offensive patterns of the opponent and directs traffic for the defense. He spots a clue to the play by the archrival Green Bay Packers.

Mike pushes himself to the limit every day, as here in the weight room of Halas Hall.

Facing monstrous offensive linemen every week forces Mike to be in top condition and totally prepared. He tries to avoid the grasp of a Pittsburgh Steeler.

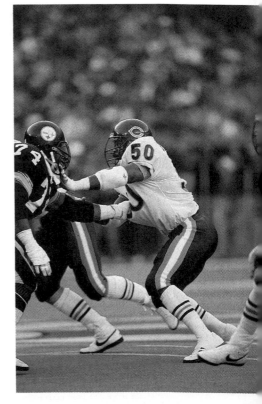

The dangling chin strap says Mike is between plays, studying the offense.

Mike is rarely surrounded by such soft characters as these promotional bears.

Fans of all ages crowd around for a glimpse, a photo, or an autograph at the Bears' Lake Forest, Illinois, training facility.

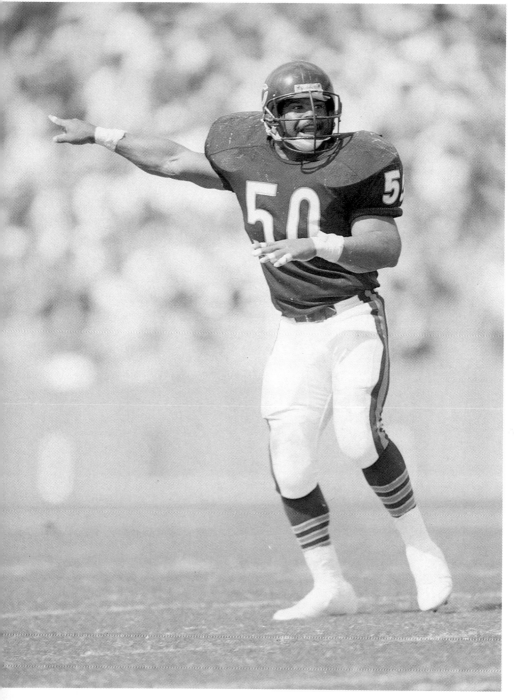

Choreographing the defense is the major part of Mike's game every
week.

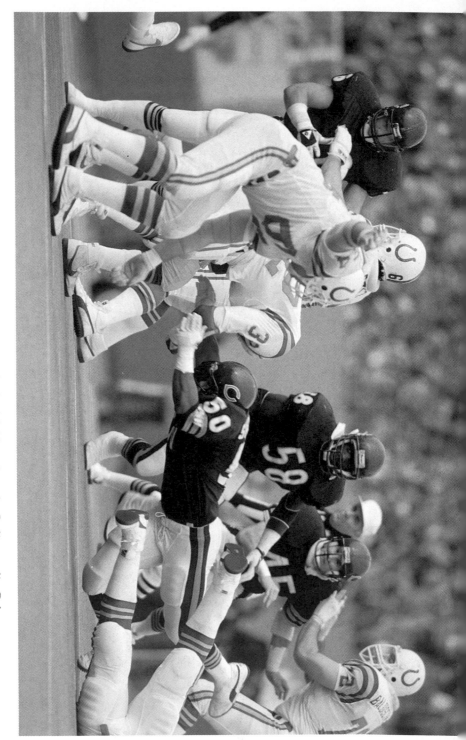

A typical Singletary play, Mike dives into the backfield against the Indianapolis Colts before Eric Dickerson can start upfield with the ball. Looking on are Bears Wilber Marshall (58) and Gary Fencik (45).

9

Rebuilding

I had had tough times in my life. When I was twelve I lost my big brother to a car accident. He had become a sort of father to me after my own father had left my mother and us for another woman. Here my father had been a preacher and so rigid and strict that we weren't allowed to wear shorts—even in gym class. Anything other than praying or reading the Bible was considered sin. And then he leaves us and the ministry for a woman.

That was a hard, hard time.

But having wounded the woman I loved, that was even worse. I had found the person I knew God had given me, and we could build a life together that would be wonderful. Yet because of my sin, and because it had taken me so long to own up to it, I had put a wedge between us that could have split us apart.

I didn't know how it would turn out. It was as if Kim were raw and sore and fragile from her pain. My injury to her lay deep behind her eyes, and nothing we did or said for weeks could erase it from our minds. She couldn't know the depth of my resolve. She would have to be convinced that I meant business. I would be not only what she had thought I was before I had told her the truth, but I would also be more. I wanted to be a man of God. She deserved a husband who kept his promises, who put her first, who was faithful to her and loved her and nurtured her.

It was not something that could be rushed. She could no more simply believe me and settle into a loving relationship again than a person could come home from heart surgery and start working out. A long period of healing was necessary. She had every right to watch me, to examine me. I had proved unworthy of her trust, and no amount of promising and the turning over of new leaves would bring it back. I had to earn it over the long haul.

I didn't know what to do other than to try to love her as Christ loves his church. That was my command from Scripture, and that meant being willing to die for her. If I never had been before, I was now. I included her in every decision. If I had a trip out of town and she wanted to come along, I didn't bristle or accuse her of not trusting me. I didn't insist that my business dealings were private and that I could handle them alone. I welcomed her.

I felt a transformation in my heart. I was empty of myself and God could now really begin a work in me.

By having let go of my bitterness toward and hatred of my dad and having confessed to my wife, I felt a transformation in my heart. I was empty of myself and God could now really begin a work in me. I had always thought I had received Christ into my life during that traumatic twelfth year, but now I'm not so sure. I had become religious, but I had little evidence of God's work in me. Now God was filling the void in me that had for so long been filled by my ego, my sin, by the world. To this day I'm not entirely sure what happened, but I know I became a new man.

I became vulnerable and sensitive. In the past, if my wife said something that offended me, I would not admit it. No one could reach me. I was a rock. Now I had to tell her. I was open and honest. She would see me cry, hear of my worries and fears and hopes and dreams. I began to pray with her, to read Scripture with her, to talk to her constantly. We went to church together as often as she wanted, because I wanted that now too. I was finished running from God. I was running to him.

Strangely, this whole experience allowed us to start over. It freed me from having to act perfect, and it

Strangely, this whole experience allowed us to start over. It freed me from having to act perfect, and it freed Kim from feeling as if she didn't have her act together.

freed Kim from feeling as if she didn't have her act together. Now we both knew the truth. I take my hat off to her. She could have left me many times over, but she was a woman of character, of depth. I live here. I know what I have. Kim loves God, she loves me, and she loves our children. She makes our house a home, and there's no place on earth I'd rather be.

There was a worse part of the ordeal. Just when enough time had passed that it wasn't constantly on our minds, I would sense that she was warming a bit. She hadn't been cold to me on purpose. It was just that she couldn't bring herself to pretend that everything was okay, that nothing was wrong, that we were as close and trusting as we had always been. When trust is betrayed, deep scars remain. But she would greet me in the morning, ask me how I was doing, and look as if she was turning a corner. I would have remembered something I hadn't told her yet. She could tell.

"I need to tell you something else," I'd say. "Would you rather I didn't?"

I could see the cloud in her eyes. "No, Mike. You know I want it all."

And I would tell her. And she would cry. And I would feel as miserable as she did. I racked my brain to remember everything; I wanted to get everything in the open once and for all. Every time something new would come to mind, we would start again. Pain. Regret. Tears.

One of the biggest problems in our society today is that we believe what we see on television. Everything works out inside of thirty minutes or an hour. Life isn't that way. We need to humble ourselves, to commit to doing things right. It's great to be proud, but eventually the pride has to go. Mine sure did. I had been humbled beyond belief. I had been broken. That's the only way to be used of God. He cannot use our pride. He would not force his way into my proud life. Only when I was at the end of myself and saw myself for what I was could He begin a real work in me.

The counterfeit was leaving my life and the real truth was coming in. I filled my mind and heart with the truth of God, the Word of God. Finally I had something to stand on for the first time in my life. I knew I was in Christ, and I knew who the enemy was. I finally discovered what grace was. I had been forgiven and given a second chance, even when I didn't deserve it.

Still, understandably, Kim was having trouble trusting me. She told me so. I prayed about it and thought about it, and then we had a talk. I told her, "I need you to understand that I'm not afraid of you. I'm not afraid of your leaving me. I'm not afraid of anything you could possibly do except to stop loving me. Because if you still love me, we will be together eventually. All I can do is to live my life as unto the Lord. I'm going to love you as unto the Lord. You wouldn't want a husband who was afraid of you and worried about what you were going to think. I don't want to worry if I'm a few minutes late that I'm going to have to face you and explain. I'm going to be a man, and we're going to stand together. We're going to be one. We'll make our decisions together.

"If I'm gone for more than one day, you're coming with me. When I talk on the phone, I'll tell you who I'm talking to. I'm going to let you know where I am and what I'm doing, but not because I'm afraid of you or afraid you're not going to trust me. It's because I know you have a right to know and because I know God wants me to do that. I know that the most important thing for our marriage is that we are pure, clean, and holy. To do that, I'm going to serve you. Not because I answer to you, but because I answer to God, and it's what he wants. If you don't trust me, I understand. I'm not worried about that, because in time you will. It's not coming from me but from the Lord."

Seven or eight months after my confession I felt as if we started to get back on an even keel. I think it became obvious to her that something miraculous had taken place in my life. I was a new person. She had still been hurt deeply, and I will live with that regret my whole life. But eventually my commitment and resolve began to win her back, to earn her faith and trust. Though it would be a years-long process, the relationship started to thaw then.

She had had a choice. She could have stayed, if that's what the Lord was telling her to do. Or she could have left and told the press what a scoundrel I was. She had every right to do that too. But she had too much class. I deserved whatever I got. But God was dealing with her as well. She was growing as I was growing. There's probably no way she could have dealt with the situation without God, so her knowledge of him was building also.

If she had simply told me she was over it, that it had been painful but she was past it now, I would have known it was not authentic. I would have known she was denying her real pain and trying to put it behind her before she had really dealt with it. I knew the healing process was going to be long and tough, and I only prayed that once we were past it, we would begin to build from there.

There are still times when I almost cry to think of what I put her through, but in many ways I would not trade what that ordeal did for our marriage. We became real for the first time in our relationship. No more games. No more pretending. There were no longer any false images to live up to. We both knew what we had gotten into. She was everything I had hoped she would be and more, and I was nothing like what she thought she had married.

I'd like to think that in the years since then, I have become more like the man she thought she married. In fact, since God has been the one doing the work in me, I know I'm more than what she would have had, had she married the man she thought I was. She may have thought I was spiritual, but she also knew I was private and moody. We had been anything but best friends.

We began to build a best friendship. We talk all the time, and I depend upon her counsel. Slowly she has learned that I am as committed to her and to our relationship as I am to my relationship with God. And I am just as determined to keep that fresh and alive as I am to be fit and prepared as a football player. I am happy to say that Kim's and my relationship is deeper and happier and more honest today than it has ever been. It is certainly more rich and rewarding than I ever deserved, but that is true of so much in my life.

Kim kept encouraging me to give Willow Creek time, and I have grown to love it. It hasn't been perfect, but it has become the place for me. There came a time when it seemed that the emphasis was more on positive mental attitude than on the Word of God, and I became concerned. We prayed for the church and for Pastor Bill Hybels. I worried because it seemed we were hearing more of a Robert Schuller or a Norman Vincent Peale type of an approach. I'm not saying either of those are bad. They aren't. I grew up watching and loving Robert Schuller and reading Norman Vincent Peale's books. They have meant a lot to me. But at my church I wanted a more straight-Bible approach.

It seemed to me that we began hearing a tired man. A man who was leaning toward the humanistic a little more than to the Word. It bothered me a lot. I told Kim, "Something is going to have to happen soon, because I don't care where I am or how much I care for Bill Hybels, if I'm not hearing the Word of God, it's time to go."

The very next Sunday, Bill had an important message. He said the Lord had been convicting him about his sermons. He said from now on he would be preaching straight from the Bible, that it was the only honest thing he could do before God, regardless how it went over with everybody. Kim and I glanced at each other and smiled. He was saying, in effect, that he didn't care about attendance or who might get their feelings hurt, he was going to preach the Word.

We knew we had found our church home. We can't ask for more than a pastor who is sensitive to the leading of the Lord in his own life. With our choice of a church settled and our marriage renewed, we set about to stay best friends. I found myself telling her everything and seeking her advice on everything. She is such a natural judge of character that I have used her to save me many times from business deals that might have blown up in my face.

I'll be close to some deal that could potentially make us some good money, and she'll say, "Mike, I don't feel right about this guy. I just don't trust him." That's all I need to hear. I don't try to talk her into it, or stick up for the guy, or do any more investigation. I'm out of there right now. For whatever I've lost on those deals, I know I've been saved from a lot worse.

Once we had begun to rebuild, we started to keep our relationship on a daily basis. I didn't want anything to get a foothold that could tear us apart. We share our most intimate thoughts and feelings on every level and every subject. We talk about everything, whether it's something we're both concerned with or not. We discuss and plan how we will raise our kids (we now have two girls and a boy). We don't want them to just slide along. We work at planning activities that will be fun, that will encourage talking and listening, that will impart spiritual values. We have to learn how to be a family and practice it. I want them to grow up to be godly adults. That will not happen by accident.

I even worried about how honest to be in this section of the book, for their sakes. But if learning that their dad suffered for his failures will keep them from falling into the same trap, it will be worth it. If nothing else, maybe it will encourage them to be honest with themselves and before God, admitting their weaknesses and depending upon him.

I insist on our kids doing what we say. I believe in discipline and honoring father and mother. The Bible says that people who honor their parents will be blessed and have a good life. I don't tolerate any ignoring of what we say or any talking back. My kids know I love them, and part of that love is expecting them to do what's right. I let them be kids, and we have a lot of fun together.

I also try to be an example to them of appreciating their mother. We don't tell her every meal is great because then she would know we were just saying it. We tell her we appreciate everything she does for us, and when a meal is outstanding, we let her know. I know a lot of wives and mothers feel unappreciated, and I'm sure Kim does too sometimes. But I want to change that in our home. Relationships start with sensitivity and love. With God at the center of our marriage and our family, we should be the most loving and sensitive of all.

Relationships start with sensitivity and love. With God at the center of our marriage and our family, we should be the most loving and sensitive of all.

We tell each other we love each other many times each day. We never get tired of saying that or hearing it. It's true. God gave my family to me. He gave me Kim as my mate. We have the greatest time. We laugh. Our home is everything I've ever wanted. God has granted my wish to be married to a wonderful woman who has become my best friend, and to have great children. That I really enjoy. When I'm away, I can't wait to get home.

The biggest trouble Kim and I have is when we don't get time for prayer together in the morning. When that happens, something always goes wrong. We get on each other's nerves, start an argument, and then stop. We track it back and realize we didn't start the day right, praying together, worshiping God together, loving each other. The only solution is to pray together right then and there. Boom, the tension, the disagreement is gone, and we start again.

It's great when the whole family gets together in the morning for prayer. I start by praying for Kim, thanking God for her and for all she does for us. Then I pray for the children, Kristen, Matthew, Jill, and the ones to come. I thank God for their uniqueness and individuality. I pray for their future spouses, that they'll remain sexually pure, that they'll become men and women of God. I pray for myself that God will give me the strength and wisdom to always do the right thing, to make right decisions for the family, not based on emotion. I also pray that I will remember that I represent my family in public, not just my immediate family, but also my parents and brothers and sisters.

We pray for friends who are going through rough times, for their children, for different guys around the league. Sometimes my prayers are long. I can really get going. But every day is different. Then Kim prays, and then the children pray. Sometimes we simply thank God for another day and an opportunity to obey him. Then we all kiss and hug each other and start the day.

Prayer is no magic formula, but the days sure go better when we begin them that way.

One night a week we have Family Night, where we

sit down and talk about what we like and what we don't like about what's been happening around the house. We find out what's been going on with everybody and how God has been working in each life during the week. If there's anything new, anything we should be thankful for, we want to hear it. Some of those times can really be touching. Then we have popcorn and show a video for the kids. After they go to bed, Kim and I might watch a favorite movie.

On Date Night, Kim and I go out together alone. We try to find a restaurant with a quiet, private corner where we won't be bothered. There we continue being honest with each other. I often try to ask her how I'm doing, what I can do to improve the relationship. Of course I'm hoping that she can't think of anything, that she'll say I'm doing everything just right.

But she knows me better than that. She knows I want her to be honest even if it hurts, and then I fight not to become defensive. I don't turn the guns on her and start correcting her. I listen, and I hurt a little, and I resolve to do what I can to do better. She deserves that. And most of all, it's what God wants of me. He's still doing a work in my heart and life, and I have to stay out of the way and let him do it.

PART FOUR

On Making It

10

The Real Man and the Feminist

I'm the old-fashioned, door-opening, chair-pulling-out, treat-a-lady-like-a-lady kind of a guy that the dyed-in-the-wool feminist loves to hate. But you know what? I'm on their side. I really am. I know that to a woman who has been mistreated, those courtesies look demeaning and condescending. It's as if we big, hot shot males are doing them a favor and treating them as if they are subservient.

I'm no male chauvinist by a long shot. I believe we

I believe we have the women's movement today because we don't have enough real men.

have the women's movement today because we don't have enough real men. And only real men are going to make it in this world. To be a true success, a man has to be real. Women look around and feel that if this is what a man is, we don't have much to work with. And it's true. If all men have to offer is talk about how good they are in bed and what a great time they have with other guys, women don't have much to look forward to.

Men took the Scriptures and went too far. They took a man's role of headship and took it as license to rule as a superior. But man's headship was supposed to be patterned after Jesus' style of leadership: servanthood. He said that he who would be the leader should be the servant of all. He never said to keep your wife barefoot, pregnant, and in the kitchen. The Word of God is the same yesterday, today, and forever. It teaches that a man is supposed to love his wife as Christ loved the church.

Too many men read the verse about wives submitting to their husbands and misread it to say that a man has the right to subject his wife. It doesn't say that. The whole passage implies that if a man loves his wife in a godly, selfless, servant-like way, she will *want* to submit to his authority. I know that very word *authority* jars the feminist and she asks, "Why should any man be in authority over me?"

If a man exercised his authority in the way it is outlined in the Bible, a woman would not resent it. She would find herself served. She would find her needs met. She would have her say, be able to exercise her gifts, not be pushed back and ignored and treated like a second class citizen. God's design for marriage is for husbands to love their wives as Christ loved the church and for wives to respect their husbands. Christ loved the church enough to die for it, and that kind of love is worthy of respect.

I see men treat women in such shameful ways that it disgusts me. I hear them tell their wives or girlfriends what to do, where to stand or sit, to shut up, to go over there, to leave them alone. It's sad. And it's wrong. It's no wonder the feminist movement had to happen. Every man had to be awakened to how he let things get out of hand.

One night I was really studying and praying about what true love was. Kim was getting ready to go to bed, and I told her I'd be along later. I read 1 Corinthians 13 and really got my eyes opened. What a passage! I know it's very familiar, but if you can look at it as if you've never seen it before, it'll open your eyes. I grew that night, just reading that and realizing what it meant. I realized I had a lot of growing to do, and I still do. I'm still trying to be the man God has called me to be. It's a life-long process.

Though I speak with the tongues of men and of angels, but have not love, I have become as sounding brass or a clanging cymbal. And though I have the gift of prophecy, and understand all mysteries and all knowledge, and though I have all faith, so that I could remove mountains, but have not love, I am nothing. And though I bestow all my goods to feed the poor, and though I give my body to be burned, but have not love, it profits me nothing. Love suffers long and is kind; love does not envy; love does not parade itself, is not puffed up; does not behave rudely, does not seek its own, is not provoked, thinks no evil; does not rejoice in iniquity, but rejoices in the truth; bears all things, believes all things, hopes all things, endures all things. Love never fails. But whether there are prophecies, they will fail; whether there are tongues, they will cease; whether there is knowledge, it will vanish away. For we know in part and we prophesy in part. But when that which is perfect has come, then that which is in part will be done away. When I was a child, I spoke as a child, I understood as a child, I thought as a child; but when I became a man, I put away childish things. For now we see in a mirror, dimly, but then face to face. Now I know in part, but then I shall know just as I also am known. And now abide faith, hope, love, these three; but the greatest of these is love. (1 Cor. 13:1–13)

How can a husband or a husband-to-be read that truth and not have it change how he treats his loved one? All I could think of was how many times I had carelessly used the word *love*. To use the word properly, you must have a certain level of maturity. You must be responsible. You must have character. Love is time. Love is action. It's easy to say I love you, but what does it mean? I have counseled my teenage niece about guys who tell her they love her. I go through the motions and do the act. I even mimic the dialect, because I want her to know how guys will talk to her and she should talk to guys.

I say, "Hey, mama, wha's happenin'. You and me could make it together. I'd love to be with you. I'd love to be with you in a special way. I know it's early in our relationship, but I'm in love with you."

And I tell her to say, "So, what does that mean?"

"Well, uh, it means I love you, girl."

And I want her to say, "The greatest act of love ever was Jesus Christ giving his life for me. Is that what you're talking about? Is that what you're prepared to do?"

"Well, hey, baby, let's not get carried away."

It really gives you something to think about. Love is kind. Love is patient. Love is not easily angered. Love believes all things. My wife exhibited that love when she forgave me and heard me say I would be faithful to her forever.

Too many people say love is impossible to understand or define. Love is action. A real man will love a woman the way the Bible says to. The most militant feminist would not condemn a love like that.

I would never say that I am the definition of what a real man is, but I'm not ashamed to say I'm working toward it. I want to be the best man I can be, and before it's over I'm trying to come close. A real man will treat his wife right. He will be a servant rather than a master. He will do the right thing because it's the right thing. He will give a hundred percent no matter what he's called upon to do.

How will a man know when he's a real man? When he seeks to serve.

And how will a man know when he's a real man? When he seeks to serve. When he can sit down with his wife and honestly look to fulfill her needs before his own. He should ask, "What can I do for you?"

Society says a man should find a gorgeous wife who will take care of his needs, make him happy, and serve him. She becomes part of his orbit, makes him proud, and he gives her everything he thinks she wants. But she's miserable. She's in second place. He can't put her first because that goes against everything he feels and has been taught. Just like with everything else God made perfect, the world has flipped this around. There's a counterfeit of the real thing being sold on the market, and it's called lust.

It's exciting. It looks good. It's even satisfying for a while. But it's not true love. It's backwards. It fulfills *our* desires first, even at the expense of the person we're supposed to love. There is a big difference, and we men need to learn and know it. Lust takes, for our benefit. Love gives, for the benefit of the one we love.

There's a big difference between loving our children and spoiling them too. We had promised our kids we would take them to the circus when we got back from a long cruise. They had missed us. We had missed them. But our flights had been delayed and traffic from the airport had been bad. We got back a half day later than we expected and didn't have time to unwind and unpack and get settled. The kids, of course, were ready for us to fulfill our promise.

It would have been easy to try to pacify them with gifts and more promises. But they would not have understood. If they had been adults, we might have been able to plead for a rain check. But what would that say to a child? That would say we don't keep our word. That they are not as important as our comfort.

Exhausted, we changed and took the kids to the circus. They were the perfect age for it, and though we would rather have been home in bed, we're glad we didn't miss the looks on their faces. They were fascinated and talked about it all the way home. When we finally dropped into bed we were glad we had kept our word and proved our love. Anything else would have been counterfeit and self-serving. Parents who really love their children keep their word. Real men keep their word too.

A father has to be careful of his promises, because a real man will follow through. There must be a careful balance between centering your whole existence around your kids and nurturing them properly. A well-adjusted child will know that there are times when he or she cannot be with his parents, when Daddy or Mommy have to work. The key is priorities. If you set a date with your child and something comes up at the office, you'd better see if you can postpone the office business. Otherwise, you're telling the child exactly where he fits in your life.

Parents need to be careful to not build their whole lives on their children, because one day those children will be gone. They will find husbands and wives to devote themselves to, and you will be left with each other. Be sure to spend enough alone time with each other now so that you won't have to get reacquainted later.

A real man is a man of integrity. That means going all out in everything he does. When he says something, you can count on it, take it to the bank. If I say I'm going to do something, you can consider it done. The first time I violate that, my credibility is shot. Our reputations are only as good as our last performances.

Unless the real men of this country—and there aren't many left—come together and align themselves under God, we're headed for catastrophe. God is looking for men who will obey and be what he wants them to be. He wants men who know how to honor and respect women, who will treat women in such a way that they don't resent us but esteem us.

A real man will deny himself the luxuries of life for

> *God wants men who know how to honor and respect women, who will treat women in such a way that they don't resent us but esteem us.*

his family. He may turn down a promotion that would mean a lot more dollars but would also cost him precious time with his family.

A real man will love his wife so much and make it so obvious that it will give his kids a sense of security. I know what it's like to see a husband and wife split and see a family fly apart. Something dies in a kid when that happens. And don't fake it. You can't fool a kid by staying together just for him. There has to be true, real love there.

Dennis Gentry, one of my good friends on the Bears, lost his mother when he was a child, maybe a little younger than I was when my parents split up. Dennis was one of nine kids who was raised by his dad and his grandmother. His dad had been working at a television station, but he quit that to open his own landscaping business. That way all the kids could work together and be with each other all the time. His dad was also a minister, and four of those kids are ministers today. All the kids went to college and most of them graduated. Dennis Gentry's dad was a *real* man.

My business partner, Sparky Beckham, is another man's man. He's an investor, but he also cares about individuals. He was once involved in a development deal in a third world country, and when the whole thing blew up on him he spent years paying off his investors. He could have filed for bankruptcy or found some loophole like so many do. But he decided the only right thing to do was to pay people back. That's integrity. That's a real man.

The Bible is full of real men. Abraham, Moses, David, Joseph, Daniel. I also love the story of Shadrach, Meschach, and Abednego. They survived in a fire so hot it killed the guard who threw them in it, because they were true to God. Not even their clothes or hair were singed!

I have to say Daniel and Joseph are two of my favorites. They had integrity and stood for what was right in the face of all odds. Daniel trusted God to protect him from hungry lions because he refused to pray to another God. Joseph said that what others meant for bad in his life, God meant for good. There are so many things in my life I would love to have the chance to do over. But God can take those failures and screw ups and turn them into ministries.

Even what I went through during my engagement period and early marriage has become a point of identification with my teammates. Every once in a while I'll have the opportunity to talk to a Bear or a player on some other team or even someone outside my arena about marriage, family, children, relationships. I think people need to know that I can relate. I remember what it's like to be single, feeling that you have to get all your fun and games out of the way before marriage. But I've learned that if you can't be faithful when you're dating, you're not likely to change when you're married. Habits are easy to form but difficult to break.

They're shocked when I say, "Man, I know exactly what you're talking about because I was there once." Their eyes get big and they want to know what happened and whether our marriage survived it. I remind them that Jesus Christ died on the cross for that sin too. As painful as that ordeal was, God meant it for good in the long run.

It would be a lot easier for me to pretend I've never had a problem. I could maintain my image as the strong man, the old spiritual guy. But who would that help? I would not be a real man if I did that.

For some reason men find it much harder to talk about their needs and shortcomings than women do. Often Kim and I will come home from a party where I have talked to the husband and Kim has talked to the wife. I'll say, "So-and-so seems to be doing well. He says he's busy and the business is going well. They seem to be happy."

And Kim will say, "Is that right? Well, so-and-so's wife had her head on my shoulder crying most of the night about their debts and the tough time they're going through—and he refuses talk about it."

I don't know what it is about that male pride and ego, but it's clear that too many men have not yielded those to God. Too many fathers give their kids the impression that they never did anything wrong when they were young, or that they do nothing wrong now either. Kids grow up thinking they're following in the footsteps of a perfect person, so anything they do that's out of line is an embarrassment to the family tree.

If a dad would just once say, "Yeah, I got sent out in the hall once myself" or "I know what it's like to want to look at those kinds of magazines too," he'd blow his kid's mind. The child would learn something and start to change and grow. With dads being afraid to be honest and vulnerable, kids learn to hide their faults until they get caught. Then they get lectured on what rotten people they are when in fact they're just normal kids who need God's forgiveness.

It would be a tragedy if my kids grew up knowing only that their dad was a good football player and husband and father. If they thought I expected them to live every minute of their lives the way they have seen me live as they grew up, they would be frustrated and devastated if they ever failed. I want them to know what they didn't see, when I failed miserably and only came out of it by the grace of God. And you know what? I'm still fighting to stay above water, with His help.

As they get older and able to understand, I'm committed to being open and honest with them. I want them to know of my mistakes so they can avoid them. I also want them to know of my mistakes because they will make their own, and I don't want them to feel they are the first person in the family to fall.

Just like I do with teammates, I want to be able to sit with my kids and tell them some of the things I have done. Not to glorify sin. Not to justify it. Not to say everybody does it so it must be okay. Rather, because I'm not proud of it and because I don't want them to feel unique. Most of all, I want them to know that by the grace of God, he brought me through it and out of it, and he can do the same for them.

11

What It Takes

I've already mentioned ob-
session as a key to success in any profession. Mine
started in a negative way. I can remember, at four
years old, hanging around the construction sites
where my dad worked. I would stand there with my
thumb in my mouth, and he would send me to get
him various tools. I'd pull that thumb out and tell
him, "Someday I'm gonna be a boss man." He'd
laugh and threaten to smack me if I didn't hurry up.

One thing I knew for sure: I didn't want to do that work unless I was in charge.

Then, when I got over all my childhood illnesses and could finally join in with the other kids in sand-lot football, I discovered a sport I loved. There weren't many sports I didn't love, but this one was special. I was rough and tough and was willing to work at it. That, combined with watching the Dallas Cowboys on TV, started my dream. There was nothing I would rather do than watch the Cowboys, unless it was imitating Roger Staubach and the rest of them in a lot somewhere.

It wasn't really that long ago that I was nine or ten, living in an 1,800-square-foot home in Sunnyside with six boys in one room and four girls in the other. Some summer nights were so hot you couldn't sleep in the bed. You had to crawl down and let the hard floor cool your body, hoping the roaches would leave you alone. If the attic fan went out, as it often did, we were in real trouble. There was nothing to draw air through the house and we'd have to open the windows and doors. Then you had to at least have a sheet between your sweaty body and the mosquitoes, no matter how hot it got.

There were tough times at home, but don't get me wrong. I had many happy memories I cherish to this day. But I wanted out of there. We all did. I know I couldn't have been the only kid in that family with dreams. There are days now when I will come downstairs in the middle of the night and go into my office and stare out at the stars. I'll say, "Lord, why me? I thank you so much, but why me?"

Sometimes I think I know why. All kinds of things went into making me the person I was. Being the youngest of ten, being sickly, being brokenhearted over my parents' breakup, losing two brothers, one who had begun to raise me when my dad left, listening to my mother everyday. All that contributed. I grew up in a church where maybe it was too strict and maybe I didn't understand a lot of it, but I sure knew the difference between right and wrong. I had no excuses there. Some of the leaders in my life were not the best examples sometimes, and I suffered from that. They lacked consistency in their Christian walk. When you're young and immature, it's easy to get confused by what you see when it conflicts with what you hear. I realized that what happened between my mom and dad was sad and unfortunate, but God holds those cards. He can still salvage a bad situation. I'm still their son, and I love them both. I can't use my past as a crutch for not succeeding in life. When I meet the Lord face to face someday, he isn't going to ask me about my life. I have to be able to stand before a holy God and give an account for my relationship to Jesus Christ.

I had the opportunity to watch my brothers and sisters grow up before me. I saw their failures and their successes. I could see their strengths and weaknesses, and I could pick and choose what to pattern my life by. I saw some of them get opportunities they let slide by. Some had a little college but dropped out for various reasons. Others slipped into the neighborhood curse of thinking the world owed them something. That's an easy thing to do. I remember wondering why we had to live that way. Why did I have to share a bed with two brothers? Why didn't I have brand-name clothes like other kids at school? Why couldn't I have a car when I was a senior? Those were dangerous "whys." Thank God I got out of that train of thought. That's the kind of thinking that can paralyze you. The success in my life could have just as naturally happened to some of my sisters and brothers, but by the grace of God I came out of it. I love my brothers and sisters dearly and would do anything I could to help any one of them. If they wanted to go back to college, start a trade, or whatever, I would help. But there's one thing I will not do, and that's give handouts. It's never wise to just hand something to someone. I deal in real problems, not the symptoms. Charity would demean them and would do neither of us any good.

As soon as I learned to read, I devoured self-help books. I read Robert Schuller and Norman Vincent Peale, and I let the principles of positive thinking and dreaming and visualizing, and goal-setting work on my mind. I didn't know what I wanted to be, but I knew it would be something special and that I would be great at it. I knew this with all that was in me, and I told myself I would pay any price. If I was supposed to be a doctor, I would study and learn. If I was supposed to be a professional athlete, I would work hard and give it my all.

Ask anyone on the street the secret to success in a given field and he'll likely tell you the same as anyone else would. Know what you want. Find out what it takes. Study, learn, set goals, go after it. Focus. Don't be defeated by one defeat. Don't get discouraged. Don't let anyone talk you out of it. Be willing to accept criticism and to put up with people who make fun of you or who don't understand. Keep your eye on the prize and be obsessive about it.

We all know, but so few of us are really willing to pay that price. What can I tell you? I was willing. Before I even knew what I wanted to be, I knew I would be willing. Even today, not knowing which direction to go when my pro football career is over, I know I will be great at whatever I choose.

I know how that sounds. Who does this Singletary think he is? Believe me, I know who I am. I know that everything I have and everything I've done has been because of the grace of God. But in his mercy he gave me a mind and a spirit and a will and a body, and He instilled in me the determination to take no

> *God in his mercy he gave me a mind and a spirit and a will and a body, and He instilled in me the determination to take no short cuts.*

short cuts. That has paid dividends I can't even count. Anybody of any age who wants to accomplish something can do it. I believe that with all my heart.

If you think it will be easy, you won't succeed. If you need things to fall in place for you, you'll fail. If you're counting on luck or breaks or fortune, it won't happen. If you think you can get something for nothing, you're mistaken. No, it isn't easy. It isn't common. But the prize is right there on the shelf. The price tag is on it. The requirement is all of yourself. Are you willing, or are you content to just dream? Do you want to simply long for something that could have, should have, would have been, or are you willing to pay the price?

I was willing, and I am still willing, and that has made all the difference. If I go into broadcasting or business or working for someone, I will give my whole self to it. I will start out walking, and I will make mistakes. I may even look bad. I will be clumsy

*If you think it will be easy,
you won't succeed.
If you need things to
fall in place for you,
you'll fail.*

and uneducated for awhile, but I will not quit. I will stay at it, obsess over it, and become whatever I need to become to succeed. I will be the kind of employee that I would want to have. If I ever coach an NFL team, I will have a team of guys who play every second, whether they're leading 100–0 or trailing 100–0. The prize is out there, and I wouldn't want it handed to me. That would be no fun. If it's not worth working for, living for, giving your all for, it's not worth worrying about.

I've been thinking that way since I was a child. I got wrapped up in the idea that this was America, the land where dreams come true. Not automatically. Not magically. But if you work at them long and hard enough, anything could happen. Why couldn't it happen to me? Why can't it happen to you?

My only problem back then was focus. I wanted to own my own multi-million dollar business. I wanted to be in the movies. I wanted to be famous in history. I wanted to write a book. I wanted the whole nine yards. Even after I met my wife, I was talking like that. Sometimes she'd say, "Mike, you can't do all that. Nobody can do all that."

And I'd say, "But I know I can."

I said it with such conviction that all she could do was look into my eyes and say, "You really believe that, don't you?"

I sure did. And that's why I was able to realize my dream. I certainly couldn't have if I didn't believe I could. Of all the things I learned from my mother and our hours and hours of talking, it was this: If you think you can't, you won't. If you think you can, you can do anything.

Probably because my mother was older when she had me and because I spent so much time with her, I have always loved to sit and listen to older people. I ask my wife's grandparents what it was like to grow up during the Depression. I ask her grandfather about the coal mines. I still ask my own mother about why she got married. What were the early days like, when there were only two or three kids and I was years away from coming along? Why do you do this? Why do you do that? If she ever got tired of my relentless, endless questions, she never let on. She was so tired from working three jobs, though, that it wasn't unusual for her to doze off during lulls in the conversation. I would let her sleep for a couple of hours right at the kitchen table before she had to head out to another job.

She did more than answer my questions. She would advise me. She would tell me how to be a good husband. What to do. What not to do. "Make sure you're a man who listens to his wife. Involve her in your decisions. Don't just take her for granted and not pay attention to her. Raise your kids the way you want them to be raised. Don't leave it to day care centers, to relatives, or to the TV. Teach them the things of God. Be a man, son. Be a man." I learned more about being man from my mother than from anybody else I ever met.

There was never extra money in that house. Mom gave me a dollar every morning that had to last me all day, even when I was in high school. That was lunch money and incidentals, and when it was gone, it was gone.

By the time I got to junior high school, all I needed was instruction. If I saw something new I wanted to try, I knew I could do it. I just needed to know how. I took up throwing the shot put in junior high. I got laughed at when I showed up at meets because I was the smallest guy there. These big rangy dudes would strut into the circle and heave with all their might. I would wait my turn, be warmed up, and take into the ring the technique I had learned through reading books on the sport in the library.

I worked so hard on developing my own technique that I hardly ever threw the shot. When I got into meets and put the ball in my hand, it was as if nothing was there. The laughing stopped when I won most of the meets. All this told me was that I could do anything if I paid the price. Learn it. Practice it. Work on it.

I overcame physical shortcomings with attitude, and I would hire attitude over talent any day. Quick. If I had been given the physical skills and attributes of most of the linebackers in the NFL today, I might have gotten complacent and would never have had the drive to keep reaching for higher levels. My work ethic has made the difference.

By the time I got into high school, the only kids left at home were my sister and me. We had a lot more freedom than our older brothers and sisters had had. They had curfews and restrictions and rules that about drove them crazy. I worried whether I would be allowed to play football. None of my older brothers had been able to. I decided that if I was not allowed, I would run away and live with a relative and play anyway. Nothing was going to stop me.

My mother trusted me. I had a strict rule about no girls in the house, but I had no curfew and was still in at a decent hour every night because I didn't want my mom to worry about me. I respected her that much. When I was old enough to drive she trusted me with the car when I needed it. I was proud of that beat up old Thunderbird. It didn't bother me to be seen in it.

By that time I was playing football under Oliver Brown, who had a huge influence on my life. He made me apply to my studies that same attitude I had on the field. He wouldn't let me take easy courses so I would have time to concentrate on football. He wouldn't let me become a slacker.

Coach Brown talked to me about life. He told me that when I shook a man's hand, he should know it had been shaken. Don't hurt the guy, but give him a firm grip, and look him in the eye when you speak to him. That was all part of being a gentleman.

He insisted on my being articulate. People always comment on how I sometimes sound like a college professor. Coach Brown said we should learn to express what was on our minds in clear, direct words and sentences. He couldn't stand the typical neighborhood kid who talked jive and dialect. He wouldn't let us get away with that. There wasn't any of this, "Yo, teach, wha's happenin'?" No, "Hey, man, yeah." It was, "Yes, sir, Mr. Brown," and, "No, sir, Mr. Brown." He treated you like a man and he wanted you to act like one.

Coach Brown would often come up with a new word and ask if you knew what it meant. If you didn't, you were to go look it up in the dictionary and be prepared to tell him the next time he asked. He was a big advocate of sending you to the board and telling you to write different problems and solve them. But that wasn't all. He also wanted you to explain them as you went. If it was something you should have known and didn't, he had a paddle.

The paddle was not as humiliating as standing before the class unable to handle the problems. The next time, you were ready. He got us to the place where we were volunteering to be the ones called upon to work at the board.

What I appreciated most about him, though, was that he noticed my drive and encouraged it. "Son," he would say, "you can't just squeeze by. You've got the talent, so use it. Go all out. Never go halfway. I don't want that. Give me your best every time. If you're so afraid to fail that you shorten up on giving me your best, you'll never know how good you can be."

His advice and my mother's advice went against everything in society. When so many people were sliding by, having fun and hanging out, the question was how bad I wanted to make something of myself. I would not allow my focus to change. I would not take my eyes off the goal. By high school I knew I wanted to be a professional football player, and I never once doubted that I would make it. I knew I would, because I would do whatever I had to to make it happen. I didn't doubt my ability, and no one could doubt my drive.

I've found that in running or lifting weights, the first few miles or the first few repetitions just get you to the place where you are really working. That's the way life is. If you never push it to the limit, you never really know your potential. You don't grow. In weight training, if you don't push the boundaries often enough, your muscles forget what they can do and you have to start fresh each time.

There's also the muscle of the mind, the muscle of

the heart, and the muscle of the will. When you call on any of those muscles to react, it won't be there unless it's been there before, in training, in practice.

People have asked me what would have happened if I had gone through all that and still not made it to college, didn't get a scholarship, didn't succeed. In a way, I guess, they miss the point. The person who is obsessed with making it will make it unless he permanently injures himself. When he believes that nothing can stop him, nothing will. I simply never let failure enter my mind.

Something I never did, and something I encourage young players to never do, is not to look at the odds. Forget the odds. The odds will tell you only that your chances are so slim you'd be more likely to be struck by lightning. Look at yourself instead. Look into your own heart and mind. Always call yourself a student athlete, not just an athlete. If you don't compete in the classroom too, regardless what kind of a student you are, you will not succeed.

I was not a great student, but I was the best I could be. I applied myself. I didn't take the easy way out. I studied. I knew I would be a better football player if I knew the discipline of working hard on my academics too.

That meant cutting out other things—attractive, fun, exciting things that everyone else was doing. The question is, what are you willing to give up? Your dream? Working hard on the field and in the classroom meant giving up going to the park with the guys. It mean giving up a lot of parties. It meant giving up a lot of dates. It meant not having a job and not having the clothes everyone else had. It meant extra homework, extra practice, putting in the extra time. I had to make those decisions.

If that price is too high, your dream is too lofty. You don't want it bad enough. I had a friend in high school who was six feet seven and weighed about 260. He had it all. But he didn't make the good, hard decisions. He didn't make the right choices. He wanted to hang out with the guys and go out with the girls. He wanted to be cool. He didn't have time to study the way he should have. His girlfriend did his homework, but she couldn't take the tests for him. His beautiful body never took him anywhere.

I had to continually remind myself that it was worth it, that I was doing the right thing. I remember many times walking home past former friends who would hoot and holler at me. "Singletary! Go to practice today? You aren't gonna win! All you guys are sorry players. You oughta quit! You ain't gonna get no scholarship! I'm goin' to a party tonight, Singletary! I'm gon' be with your girl."

They would laugh, and I would just keep walking. I had a dream. I knew God had given me something special. I knew that someday I would either be playing in the NFL or be the greatest physical therapist who ever lived.

Coach Brown told us not to just sit in front of the air conditioner during the off-season. We didn't have air conditioning, so that took care of that. But he didn't want us, he said, "sitting around eating ice cream and drinking pop all the time. You've got to keep working to stay in shape."

In the summer, when I got home from work my best friend Ron Williams and I would run and run and run. Then we would lift weights in my garage hour upon hour. It got to the point where about half the high school team would work out with us about three times a week. It was tough, but we did it.

Coach Brown told us not to just sit in front of the air conditioner during the off-season. We didn't have air conditioning, so that took care of that.

I was always looking for a sign from the Lord. I wanted a scholarship, even though I literally didn't know what that meant. I thought it was some kind of an honor, but everybody seemed to be looking for one, so I was too. I would pray, "Lord, if I reach six-foot-one, that means I'll get a scholarship." Then I would measure myself—not a good idea. I could stretch and reach and angle the pencil until I had convinced myself I was taller than I was. That was okay with me. It was a sign. I would get one of those scholarships, whatever that meant.

I wanted to succeed so badly that sometimes, in the night, I would awaken with the nagging feeling that I had not worked out enough that day. I would head out to the garage, crank up the music, and work some more. I would do pushups, sit-ups, isometrics, all that stuff. Sometimes I would run up and down the street in the night, sideways, forward, backward.

When I felt sufficiently worked out, I would sit on the hill and look at the stars, talking to God. I called him the Man Upstairs then, but I was sincere. "Lord," I'd say, "I know you hear me talking to you. I want to be prepared. I want to do it. I've got this dream, this goal in my mind. I want you to stand with me, to stand by me, because I'm going to give you everything I've got."

All I wanted was to play football, but I knew God could change his mind about that. He might want me to be a doctor or a teacher or something. Whatever it was, I would be ready.

12

Getting There

By the end of the football season during my senior year at Worthing High School in Houston, I was rated the third best linebacker in the state. Texas is a huge high school football state, so I felt I was right on track for college and the pros. Of course, I thought I was the best linebacker in the state, but if people thought I was third, that was okay for now.

Recruiters were after me constantly. Most were

"Mike, if we never win a championship, if we never go to a bowl game, that would not bother me as much as your walking away from Baylor without a degree."

from smaller schools; but once Baylor and the University of Texas noticed me, the other big ones came along. But they were too late. The one who got to me was Grant Teaff of Baylor University. He said, "Mike, if we never win a championship, if we never go to a bowl game, that would not bother me as much as your walking away from Baylor without a degree."

We talked more about academics than we did about football, and that was right up my alley. I had not been a great student, but it wasn't for lack of trying. The idea of a college education was a dream to me. I was not going to waste the opportunity.

Other schools offered cars and money and jobs. One even had a date waiting for me when I visited. I knew better than to accept any of those things. It scared me to death. I knew nothing came free. If my family couldn't afford it, I didn't need it. But my mother and I were the only ones who agreed I should go to Baylor. My brothers and sisters all had their favorites, some because of one fancy offer, others because of another.

Even my teachers got into the act. When they heard I was leaning toward Baylor they wanted to know if I knew what I was getting into. "That's an academically oriented institution," one told me. "You're really going to feel the pressure. You need to think hard about it because it's going to be tough."

That was supposed to be a warning? That would keep me away? No way. No more than the other recruiters when they found out I was favoring Baylor. They would immediately jump in and say, "Football will be second to academics every day at Baylor. You'll be ignored as a football player while they worry about your work in the classroom."

I asked those guys how many of *their* players graduated. "Oh, uh, I'm not sure, but it's up there. It's way up there. But we go to the major bowls, and guys who play for us get the rings, man, they get the bowl rings. And you know what that means. The pro scouts watch those bowl games."

Who were those guys recruiting for? They were talking me out of their places and into Baylor. I knew I wouldn't play football all my life, even if I went on to have a long and successful career. I promised my mother that no matter where I went I would get my degree. There would be no wavering on that. I was as determined about that as I was about my football. And I knew that if I played at Baylor we would win our share of games and get to enough bowls. I would be noticed. I wanted to go to a place where the coaches were more concerned about my education and my degree than they were about football.

I also planned to learn everything I could, ask every question that arose, and educate myself in the business of money. Even then I had a sense that I

I knew I wouldn't play football all my life, even if I went on to have a long and successful career. I promised my mother that no matter where I went I would get my degree.

would one day have to manage larger than normal amounts of income, and I wanted to do it myself. It was more than a matter of pride. It was also a matter of privacy and safety. I didn't want to get ripped off. If I wind up broke at the end of my career, I'll have no one to blame but myself.

Baylor was where I wanted to go, and I was willing to pay the price. On my first recruiting trip there I learned from another prospect just what a scholarship was. I couldn't believe it. They would pay for my tuition, my room and board, and all my books and fees for four years. No wonder everybody was after a scholarship! That took some getting used to, but apparently I was the only person who hadn't known that. I would tell people and they'd say, "Of course! What did you think a scholarship was?" I didn't want to tell them I thought it was something you framed and hung on the wall.

Assistant Coach Corky Nelson was honest with me. "We've got two linebackers already who can knock your block off. I can't promise you'll get a lot of playing time."

"I'll get plenty of playing time if I get the opportunity," I said. "Are you telling me I won't get the chance to show you what I can do?"

"Oh, you'll get your opportunities. I just want you to know we're deep at linebacker and you'll have to wait your turn."

"All I want is a chance." I was not going to be denied. It was as simple as that. Eight games into the season I became a starter and my sophomore through senior years I was the defensive player of the league. I broke sixteen helmets during my career there.

There were no mice or roaches at Baylor. And there were three square meals a day, all you needed and wanted. No way the food would be as good as my mom's cooking, but there would be plenty of it. The dorms were clean and nicely furnished, the campus beautiful. You have to imagine what it was like for a kid like me to see that and to dream of going there. I began building a rock-solid resolve. I was going to take advantage of every opportunity. I would do everything just right. I would get up at a certain time, be at the cafeteria for meals on time, go to every class, ask every question, take every note, do all my homework, write all my papers, study for every test, work out, and play football as hard as I could. Man, I was ready.

I could hardly believe it when I saw athletes taking it easy. Some of them didn't like how hard the late summer practices were, so they just quit and left. Who could give up an opportunity like that? I saw seniors drop out of school after the football season was over, waiting to get drafted. Who needed an education when the NFL came calling? Didn't they know that the average career for an NFL player lasts just a few years?

During my first practice I was so serious and intense that one of the older players got on my case. "What are you trying to do, become an all-American?"

What a question! That was precisely what I had in mind. I looked him in the eye and said, "As a matter of fact, I am." A few days later there were no jeers.

There was lots of laughter and fun in the locker room, but that was not my style. I was on a mission. I knew what I wanted to do. First was to get my degree, second was to play pro football. The guys thought I was too serious. I didn't think they were serious enough.

On the field I was so intense that I would wear myself out after just a few minutes. I would be so exhausted I couldn't get up after a play. They would come and get me, splash me with water, rest me up, and send me back in. Finally they insisted that I learn how to turn on and off the excitement. I was going to kill myself. I had to force myself to calm down between plays, to quit hyperventilating. I loved the game, but I was so excited I could hardly control myself.

All I needed to know was what needed to be done. What does it take to pass a course? What does it take to become a starter? What does it take to become defensive player of the team, the game, the league? What does it take to get noticed, to get drafted? If a coach said, "Mike, here's what it takes," you could consider it done. I wasn't going to be one of those guys who headed home when things got tough. There was nothing back in Sunnyside but a future of trouble. By the time I got to Baylor, I was gone from Sunnyside, as a place to live, forever. I had in mind a new home for my mother, and I dreamed about that

I wasn't going to be one of those guys who headed home when things got tough. There was nothing back in Sunnyside but a future of trouble.

constantly. Someday. Someday, I would be able to provide that for her.

People liked me because I became known. They wanted me to run out with them at midnight for pizza. I couldn't. I was either studying or sleeping. There were parties. I usually didn't go. I spent a lot of time in the library. That was where I met Kim, when I was a sophomore and she was a freshman. I had my books spread out enough for several people, and she was looking for a place to sit down. When she noticed I was studying math, she hoped I could help her pass one of her tough courses. She thought I was boring at first.

I really discovered how much Coach Grant Teaff believed in me and cared for me when I fell in love with Kim. We were (not surprisingly) hassled from all sides. Even people who claimed not to be prejudiced, and probably weren't, insisted that our relationship could never work. They warned us of bringing mixed children into this world, and all the other typical cautions about inter-racial marriage.

Coach Teaff had helped me make my decision to go to Baylor, which, as I look back on it, was one of the most important of my life. Now he was the guy I went to with my problems. What should I do about Kim's parents' apprehensions, and those of many people who cared about us?

He was a real man, transparent, loving, kind, and wise. He said, "Mike, whatever you need me to do, I'll do. I'll go with you to talk to her parents. I'll serve as a reference, you name it."

I told him that really what I needed was just his advice. "What would you do, Coach?"

"Hey, if you love her and she loves you, you can make it work."

There were others who told me flat out it would never work. Some of those people are Kim's and my dearest friends today. One coach told me, "If it was my daughter I couldn't handle it."

But Coach Teaff was a champ. He said, "If it were my daughter, I would be happy she was marrying someone like you, because I know what kind of a man you are. I'm for you. It's a tough situation, but you can make it work." He didn't pretend it was no prob-lem. He was honest with me and supportive. I'll never forget that.

My zealousness on the football field carried over to the classroom. I had less natural academic ability than I did athletic, so I had to work even harder in class. I was determined to understand and know ev-erything the professors were saying, and I drove them crazy. It got to the point where they would ask me to save my questions until after class. So, I would make notes of the things I didn't understand, and I would walk with them from the classroom to their offices, asking questions and taking more notes along the way.

When they had to beg off because of other commitments, I made appointments with them and spent hours with them if necessary. They would go over and over the material, and I would sit there scowling, trying to get it, trying to get the light to come on in my head. I believed if I could understand it, I would learn it. The profs admired my attitude, but I wore them out. It got to the point where some would actually pin notes to their doors saying, "Not today, Mike."

I had been given this incredible gift: four years of a university education because I happened to be a good football player. It was an opportunity of a lifetime and I was not going to squander one minute of it. Everybody thought I was too serious, too intense, no fun. I wasn't listening. Nothing could make me waver. My goals were a degree, pro football, and a house for Mom.

People often ask me to advise their kids on their football careers, but maybe I'm not the one to ask. Maybe those parents really don't want their kids to be as obsessive as I have been. Of course, if the kids are not, they probably won't make it unless they are perfect physical specimens.

I do encourage kids to be careful about weight training. And of course I'm down on steroids. They're illegal, they're unsafe, and they're going to cost a kid a price too high to pay. I lifted weights when I was a freshman and sophomore in college, but I soon realized I knew too little about it to be effective. I was building muscle, but I was also becoming inflexible. I got to such a bulkiness that I couldn't move the way I wanted to. I was still quick and fast, but not as fluid.

The next two years I concentrated on flexibility and strength, rather than on bulk. I did a lot of reading on the subject and quit lifting, concentrating more on pushups and situps. Guys would see my musculature and my strength and ask about my lifting routine.

"I don't have one," I'd say.

"Well, what do you bench?" (They still ask me that today.)

"I don't bench," I say.

I got away from weights because I was aware I didn't know what I was doing. I would ask the so-called experts, and they wouldn't tell me why I was doing what I was doing. So I quit that. I felt some muscles were hard and stiff and others were weaker. There was no balance. Once I started reading and learning how to work out muscle groups and how to lift based on what sport you played and what your weaknesses were, I began to make progress.

A lot of athletes really screw themselves up. The problem is that weights work. If you lift, you will grow. But do you know what you're doing and will it make you better at your sport? Today I have a basement full of weights. But I also have a shelf full of books on how to use them correctly. I am in the process of strengthening weak areas and improving strong ones. I want to cut my physique to right where it needs to be for the start of the football season. I'm not into a washboard abdomen or bulging veins everywhere. Looking like a body builder does not make a man a football player.

Kids can even get into trouble if they don't know how to stretch and manipulate their muscles. You see people all the time come bounding out of the house on the dead run. A jogger needs to stretch carefully first to avoid cramps and pulled muscles. There's so much to learn and to know before seriously working out. My advice to parents and to kids is to not take conditioning lightly. The danger of a kid getting inspired by a story like mine is that he might just start lifting weights that will do the wrong things to his body.

He may have all the determination and drive in the world, but if he spends hours lifting weights that are too heavy for him or doing exercises that are not right for the part of the body he wants to improve, he will only set himself back.

I don't want to see that. I want to see young people who have a plan, a dream with some sense to it. Keep that flame alive. Don't let anybody tell you you can't do it. Don't let anyone put a doubt in your mind. Not a coach, not a player, not a friend. If you've got a dream, go for it until you succeed. Just remember, take God with you.

PART FIVE

On the Current Crisis in Character

13

The Fall of the Role Model

You hear a lot of profes-
sional athletes today saying that it's unfair to put
them on pedestals. They say they never signed up to
be paragons of virtue or any kid's role model. They
say it's too much pressure.

I don't mind being a role model. I'm flattered when
people say they'd like their kids to be like me. To me,
being a role model is a heavy responsibility and a gift
from God. I accept it openheartedly. But at the same
time, I don't feel I should become more important in

a kid's life than his father and mother. Very few kids ever actually emulate their heroes. They do what their parents did. Parents are the most important role models in their children's lives, for good or bad.

To me, being a role model is a heavy responsibility and a gift from God. Parents are the most important role models in their children's lives, for good or bad.

I may be signing autographs somewhere and a single mom will come up with her son. She'll say, "I'm so glad he got to meet you because you're his hero, and he'll do what you say. If you tell him to listen to his mother and do what I tell him, he'll do it."

That's sad. I often give them both a little encouragement, but I'd rather that kid know that I'm human too. I came from a broken home too. I knew what it was to be disappointed in my father and to be raised by my mother. That mom has the toughest job because she will serve as both the father and the mother role model for that child. He may admire me and look up to me or some other celebrity, but when the chips are down, he'll pattern his life after his parents. If we've got a role model crisis in this country, it's because parents are not good ones.

Most of the role models in the sports world today are scary. I won't mention names, but you see them all the time. They're the guys who make millions of dollars before they've stepped onto the field for the first time. They wear outrageous clothes or jewelry or hairstyles. They flaunt their life-styles and are always at the edges of drugs or alcohol or wild living. They're known as party animals or woman chasers, and the more trouble they get into, the bigger they are in the eyes of kids. How cool to be a rebel, to break the rules, to be unashamed in your search for fame and glory and money and material things, and get away with it.

I already wrote about the scarcity of real men. Too many fathers are a long way from what a real man should be. They brag about everything except what it means to be a real man. They are proud of being unfaithful to their wives. They think it's cute when they get drunk or high or busted for driving recklessly. To me, when a man has to drink excessively or do drugs it's a sign he's trying to hide from something. It says he's not pleased with who or what he is. He's not happy with himself. He thinks a little booze or a little tobacco or a little dope will elevate him. But it never works. And meanwhile, kids are looking up to him.

These are the same guys who will tell you that real men don't cry. Well, I cry. Does a decade as an NFL linebacker qualify me as a real man? Then I say real men have the freedom to enjoy the full range of emotion and feeling.

I never bought that myth about a man not being allowed to cry. Soon after my brother Grady was killed and my dad was gone, I was having a problem at home. I guess I was being smart or uncooperative or something, and my mom made me do some chore anyway. I was feeling sorry for myself and I was crying. One of my older brothers noticed and jumped all over me.

"What're you cryin' for, man? Don't you know you can't cry? Men don't cry. Wipe your eyes."

I wiped my eyes and never forgot that. But I never agreed with it either. Wouldn't it be nice for a man to be caught crying by his son, when something is worth crying over? It doesn't make him less than any other man. In fact, it might make him more of a man.

My dad was a troubled, inconsistent, hard man, and I've already talked about the resentment that built in me toward him. But he was a good role model for me in many ways too. While I found myself copying his bad traits early in my marriage, and I had to get that straightened out, I have to credit him for some of my good traits too. His work ethic was as strong as anyone's I ever knew. He loved to work and was always doing it. He didn't have to be told what to do; he found something to do. Industry and persistence were his middle names.

For whatever his other weaknesses, my father was a man of integrity in the workplace. When he went to work, he gave a full day. He got the job done. He had the respect of his employers and clients because he did first class work all the time. He taught his sons to do the same. Just as I always heard from my coaches, my dad harped on us, "Whatever you're doing, do it right. Put your heart into it. Don't do half a job."

He wanted his sons to have a trade, to know how to think for themselves, to take advantage of the free enterprise system. He built our house with his own hands, starting with the master bedroom and building the rest in stages. He put in the plumbing and the electricity. We were the first in Sunnyside to have a sewer. He was very innovative, despite having only

"Whatever you're doing, do it right. Put your heart into it. Don't do half a job."

an eighth-grade education. Our garage and the rest of the house was full of books. He was self-educated.

He taught himself algebra and even other languages. He read the dictionary frequently. Dad often told me, "Son, the more you know about life, the less you have to pay somebody else to think for you."

He was too hard, too rigid, too much of a disciplinarian. Many times in a rough marriage the problems trickle down to the rest of the family. Eventually he quit practicing what he preached for a while. So he wasn't very good at raising kids when I was a child. But still I learned from him. I gleaned the good stuff and turned away from the bad. Too many people today feel trapped by the way they were raised. Why can't they just react to it? They know it was wrong, so avoid it. We don't have to be products of our upbringing. We can be products of the way we react to it.

As a kid I argued with the neighbors about whose dad was the biggest and the bravest and the toughest. Do kids still do that today? Or are fathers so busy trying to pay for the good life that they're not around enough for the kids to even know? Dads today are so busy that they're boring. Dad drives a nice car, wears a conservative suit, and shows up once in a while if there's nothing cooking at the office. How can he compete with some rock star or movie star or sports star?

My mother was a great role model for me too, never quitting, never giving up, working all those jobs to take care of her kids. We talked every day and I listened and learned. When I had been in the NFL for a few years I arranged to buy her a new house, but she refused to move out of Sunnyside. I felt pretty sorry for myself and complained to my former high school football coach.

He said, "What are you trying to do, kill your mother?"

"What do you mean?" I demanded. "I'm trying to help her out of a bad neighborhood and set her up nice."

"Don't you see the insult in that? You're telling her that her neighborhood's not good enough for you. It produced you, didn't it? It's where she's lived for decades. It's where her friends are. Why should she leave just because you want to fulfill your childhood dreams?" I didn't want to live in a nice house and have my mother live in Sunnyside.

What Coach said made sense. I asked her if I could build her a new house right in Sunnyside. She said sure, as long as it was on the same spot as the old one. So that's what I had built. She's happy, and so am I. Dad lives nearby. I try to show them how much I appreciate them both by taking care of them now. They'll never want for anything, as long as I'm alive. In spite of their problems, I esteem them both. I honor them, just like the Bible says we should.

It makes me sick to see surveys of teenagers and to find out that their most admired people are movie stars and rock stars, people like that. What about Mother Theresa or Billy Graham or Margaret Thatcher? What about Bob Hope and Sidney Poitier, if you want to admire somebody in show business? There are all kinds of role models and heroes who give of themselves and their resources to help other people. I don't understand how a kid can list as a hero a woman who basically undresses in public, ahead of someone who risks her life feeding the poor.

I guess kids have no role models at home to point out things like that to them. Whenever I can during the season and always during the off-season, I go with Kim when she takes the kids somewhere. If it's a school or preschool or church function, or if it's to the doctor or dentist, I always find that I am either the only one or one of very few fathers who ever show up. I realize I have an unusual privilege to have time off occasionally, but are other fathers *never* able to get away? Who is raising these children?

Even if I go to a function during the week where it's supposed to be family night, mostly mothers and their kids are there. And I suppose many of them are single parents, so not only is the father not at the function, he's not living at home either.

What has caused this? In the last twenty years our country has gone from America the Beautiful to America the Ugly Me-First Nation. Everything in society became free and open, and men went off to make their fortunes. The result is broken homes, men who are hung up on themselves and their careers and their incomes. They try to tell themselves they're doing it for their families, but they're losing their families in the process.

The great substitute for spending time with kids is giving them things. Parents are saying, "If I can't give you me, I'll give you this instead." The problem is, the kids aren't buying the replacement. Oh, they'll take all the parents give them, and they may even become spoiled and demanding. But they'll be the worse for it. Down deep they don't want things. They want their parents.

I grew up getting one gun and roll of caps for Christmas, and sometimes nothing at all. If Dad didn't have work, we had maybe a tree and that was it. We learned values. We discovered what was important. Today Kim and I feel so privileged that we try to teach our kids what Christmas is truly all about. When we tell our kids about other children who have nothing, they want to share some of their things with the underprivileged. They just need coaching, modeling, time, and input to become generous, others-oriented people.

Parents who think "things" are a reasonable substitute for real role modeling should look at the teen suicide rate. Suicide is second only to accidents as the leading cause of death among teenagers. Something is wrong. Something isn't working. Kids are being left alone to make their own decisions, to teach themselves about life, to fend for themselves. It's killing them.

Parents need to let their kids know that not everyone will love them. Not everyone will accept them. People can be cruel and unthinking. But a kid needs a role model to tell him that he is loved and cared about at home. No matter what happens anywhere else, there is something and someone worth living for. "God is with you and I love you, and that's all that matters." No kid who honestly believed that could ever take his own life.

I first felt genuinely needed in my family when my mother sat me down and told me I couldn't be the class clown anymore. I had been staggering along in school, having a good time and not taking much seriously. But with Dad gone and my brother dead, Mom needed me. Things began to fall into place for me. I could see with a new perspective. Life was real and serious and crucial. "You have to stand up and become the man of the house," she told me. "We really need you."

> *"You have to stand up and become the man of the house," she told me. "We really need you."*

I had a sense that without me, we were not going to survive. Do kids today get that feeling? I don't think so. I think that's why they hang out and do nothing or cause trouble. That's why they loiter in the parking lots of fast food places and in malls. They feel no sense of responsibility. They get no attention and they certainly don't feel needed. My heart goes out to them. Their parents have abandoned them to this culture.

In our home we are teaching a team concept. We are a family. Each member is important. We do things together, making projects out of chores. If we're doing a job, everybody has a role, even the littlest child. Why? Because we are a family, and families matter. Once the family deteriorates, there's little left.

Not only has society dropped the baton on this, but also no one seems willing to pick it up and get back in the race.

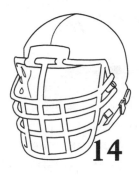

14

The Buck Stops Here

People today want to point the finger at everyone else. That never makes any sense to me. We have to take responsibility for our own actions and blame no one else for our failures. We all want to be geniuses and think of ourselves as perfect. It's so much easier to look outwardly instead of inwardly when things go wrong. When we look inside, we see things we don't want to see. Then we compare ourselves with other people and decide we're not so bad after all. We're funny people.

*We have to take responsibility
for our own actions and
blame no one else for
our failures.*

The media helps shape us. Kim and I make sure we're watching with our kids when the TV is on. Even the so-called wholesome shows, even some funny situation comedies, teach values that we don't agree with. Have you ever noticed how many comedies make the parents look like idiots? The kids always have the smart ideas and are able to pull one over on Mom and Dad. And if one parent does look good, it's usually the mother. Dad is usually a moron. That may look funny, but the overall message is sad.

Other shows make premarital sex look acceptable. Everybody's doing it. On a recent comedy I heard a young man say to a teen girl, "You mean you've never done it?" The audience found that hilarious. A virgin is something to be mocked and made fun of today. And we wonder why teen pregnancies and abortions are increasing.

When I speak to high schools and tell kids to stay away from tobacco and alcohol and drugs and sex, you can hear a pin drop. It's a challenge, and it takes a commitment. I can tell the kids want to take the challenge, but many of them have already fallen, having given in to peer pressure. They want to do the right thing, but at the same time they don't want to be out of it.

Kids are being raised on cartoons and sitcoms where it's cool to be smart and sassy. I watched "The Simpsons" with my kids, and I'm not ready to call it anti-family. It had its funny spots. But let's face it, that is an adult show. The humor is for people who understand exaggeration and satire. If kids watched it alone, they might not understand that it's a put-on. They might think it's funny to make fun of your parents and to be a smart mouth.

The parents are dumb. They don't know anything. They are worthy of no respect, and they get none.

When we complain about the kids' choices of heroes and role models, we can't blame that all on them either. We can coach them, encourage them to look at the person's private life. Sure it looks attractive when someone can fill a 70,000-seat stadium and sing for two hours, making millions of dollars. But do the songs have a good message? Is the star married, a family man, raising kids in a responsible way? Does he control himself, or is he always getting into trouble? And would the kids be so enamored with the celebrity if there was some important adult in the kids' lives who showed personal interest?

What if a teen's dad talked heart to heart with him everyday? What if that dad knew what was going on in school, who his friends were, who he thought he was in love with, what his problems were? I'm not talking about intruding and trying to tell a kid how to run his life. I'm talking about being a friend, caring, talking, listening. Then when that survey comes around about who your hero is, Dad might find himself listed above Michael Jackson or M. C. Hammer or Madonna.

Role modeling starts from the top down. We even send a message to our kids by who we elevate. Look at the people who run for President of the United States. We get more hairdos and pretty boys, it seems, than we get serious-minded people who push for a return to values. It used to be that working people held the jobs of senators and congressmen and judges. Now we have lawyers and media stars. There was a time when a lawyer was looked up to as a man of integrity. Now lawyers are the butts of jokes.

We've changed. Now we care more about who is convincing and who looks good than about who's right. We are so materialistic that we hear only what we want to hear. The guy who says the right thing will get our vote, whether he's lying or not. He bases his public statements on what the polls say we want to hear. Character and integrity are out the window. We want glamour and a nicely turned phrase.

What can we do? Is this society so far gone that it's hopeless? Have we abandoned our role model responsibilities for so long that we can't change? I don't think so. Each of us can change our own little world. Fathers who are honest with themselves will admit that we all make mistakes. We have all made bad decisions. Some of those decisions have to be reversed. If you have accepted a promotion and a transfer that takes you a step up the corporate ladder at the expense of your kids, maybe you need to think about taking a step back. More important than providing a life of ease for your kids is making sure they know you love them unconditionally.

The kids need to feel needed. They need to know that if they're not carrying their share of the load, that makes it tougher on Mom and Dad. But if everyone is doing his part and you're working together as a family, then there will be time to teach and to learn,

More important than providing a life of ease for your kids is making sure they know you love them unconditionally.

to talk and to listen, to pass on values. Your children should know their heritage. They should know about your parents and even your grandparents. They should know who your heroes are. They need role modeling, and none will be as good as you.

Kids in the ghetto find themselves looking up to pimps and drug pushers, because they're the ones who seem to have the clothes and the girls and the cars and the money. They are most likely high school dropouts, and from them kids get the idea that nothing is important but finding an angle. Get a scheme and make your mark. Kids who follow role models like that will be dead before they reach adulthood.

When role models seem to get along without knowing anything about philosophy or English or math, kids don't see why they need those subjects either. I've got a relative who is talented in music, sports, and art. He's got a good head, but he's wrapped up in the music. He barely finished high school, didn't go to college, and he's chasing his career.

I think that's fine, to a point. I'm not going to violate my own advice and try to talk him out of his dream. But he needs a base, a back-up plan, just like I did. If my football career ended today, I have knowledge and education and a degree that would open doors for me elsewhere. I learned things in college that would give me a head start on a new career.

Making it in music is a one-in-a-million proposition, but that's all right. Like I've said, he shouldn't look at the odds. But I say go to college. Get that degree. Major in music if that's your love. Know everything there is to know about music and the music business. Learn how to manage your money. Learn how to run your own company. Then you can invest in your own studio, where there's real money, whether you ever perform or not. It's not how much money you make, it's how much you keep.

Well, I'm finding out it takes time to raise kids—especially to raise them right. I compare raising a family to raising a garden. You can't just go out there and drop seeds into the ground and watch them grow. For one thing, it won't happen overnight. The soil has to be prepared, the seed nurtured, the weeds removed, constantly. Parents are with me on this already. You know exactly what I'm talking about.

The budding plant needs sun and water and attention. And it has to be the right kind. If you get frustrated with a plant and try to force it, you'll kill it. If you tell a kid he's slow or stupid or worthless, he'll believe it, and that's what he will become.

It takes a strong child to break that long cycle in a family. That's why you see abused children become abusers, adult children of alcoholics become problem drinkers or alcoholics themselves. They carry on the tradition until someone stands against it and says it's going to stop. Someone needs to say that if this family is going to have a legacy of anything but alcoholism and abuse and divorce, it's going to have to start with me and my children and a lot of grace. Stop using a bad heritage as an excuse and start using it as an example of how not to live.

My son, who is only three years old at this writing, is not too young for daily serious input from his daddy. No, I don't try to talk to him about the mysteries of the universe or the doctrines of the faith. But he already knows the Singletary Creed. He knows his daddy loves him unconditionally. He knows I make time for him and that he's an important priority in my life.

Matthew already knows how to shake hands as firmly as a three-year-old can, and he will look you in the eye when you speak to him. He's polite.

I'll ask him why he is special, and he'll tell me, "Because Jesus died for me."

Ask my daughter who made her, and she'll say, "God did."

I know they're too young to understand it all now, but someday soon they won't be. I want to have established a pattern of talking to Dad about important things, the things of God, the things of life. They need a format to express themselves, and I don't want to have the typical environment where the kids don't talk to the parents and the parents don't have a clue as to what's going on in a child's mind and life.

I'll ask Matthew, "What are you thinking?"

He'll roll his eyes and say, "I don't know."

I'll say, "You don't know? Well, I'll tell you what I'm thinking."

"What?"

"I'm thinking God gave you to me and I'm going to love you just like he does. No matter what."

"Yeah!"

If that doesn't get him talking, we'll just roll around on the floor for a while and I'll let him climb on me. Then I might get serious. "Matthew," I'll say, "do you have any idea at all how much I love you?"

He'll hold his hands about a foot apart and say, "This much?"

I'll act indignant, like he's insulted me. "Oh, man! More than that!"

He'll smile and widen his hands a little. I'll say, "Come on! It's this much!" And I'll hold my hands as far apart as they can go, then I'll wrestle him to the floor again while he giggles.

Sometimes he just comes up to me and kisses me. I'll say, "What was that for? Why did you do that?"

"Because I love you."

"You do?"

"Yeah!"

"I almost forgot!"

"You did not, Daddy!"

I want him to grow up to be a real man, and I want him to enjoy being a kid too. I love to see him with a little helmet on, running around and crashing into everything. But I will also teach him to be a gentleman. I know how I longed for that kind of attention from my dad when I was a kid. Don't think your children can live without it from you.

Somewhere, somehow, we're losing that in our society. I want my kids to grow up knowing the truth, knowing things like the fact that people are fickle. There will be people who act as if they like and respect you for yourself, but it will actually be because you are Mike Singletary's kid. That can be an advantage sometimes, but in the long run it doesn't work. I can be a hero and a well-known personality one day and be a goat and on the way out the next. Then where will your fair-weather friends be?

Very few people truly want to get to know the real me. They are content to believe what they read or see

You see how fragile and compli-
cated raising kids can be?
They need role models.
They need parents.
They need you.

or hear. My kids need to know that they, too, will have very few true friends, friends who know all about them and love them just the same. Friends are people who care about you and are there for you regardless whether your father is famous. Friends are those who want the best for you regardless what they get out of being your friend.

If the benefits or the fun of saying, "I know Mike Singletary's kid personally" all of a sudden ends, only the true friends will remain.

Your kids need to learn these lessons too. They need to be careful who they call friend, because the people they surround themselves with can make them or break them. You become like the people you associate with, so what is your plan? Do you hang with people who will lower you to their level? Or do you run with people who will be good for you and challenge you and make you a better person?

You can't please everybody. That's why my wife and I strive to teach our children the truth of the Word of God. That's all that matters. The truth will set you free. If this or that person has a problem with you, doesn't like you, doesn't accept you, that's his problem. You go on because you're right with God and right with your family.

You see how fragile and complicated raising kids can be? They need role models. They need parents. They need you.

15

What's Wrong

I know this chapter could make a man in his early thirties sound like someone twice that age, but still I have to get this off my chest. I can't believe I'm the only one seeing what's happened to America in the last few decades, but too few people are talking about it.

What was it like when you were a kid? I remember that we were more neighborly when I was growing up. If we left town, we could expect the neighbors to keep an eye on our house. I guarantee they watched it better than any watchdog would have. Nobody better step a foot in your yard while you were away or he would have to answer to the neighbors. When you got back home your neighbor would have your mail and your packages and a list of anybody who came by. If the parents had to be gone, the neighbor would even watch the kids. Try to throw a party, and the neighbors knew better than to let you. They'd mosey over and say, "Hey, is this all right with your parents?" You'd better have the right answer and proof of it, or they'd make you shut it down.

That kind of watching out for each other is almost gone now. We're not as neighborly as we used to be. Ever wonder why?

I also remember that almost everybody used to go to church on Sunday. That was the norm. Even the worst kids in the neighborhood went to church. Now if you go to church, you're in the minority. It seems hardly anybody goes. If you go to church you're seen by your neighbors as "one of those."

Something else we did as kids that I seldom see kids do today: play all day at a park or lot or field. Whatever happened to that? Don't people realize that that is where the high school, college, and professional athletes come from? When you play football or baseball for six or eight or even more hours every day, you build your body, you improve your skills, and most of all, you program your muscle and coordination to remember angles and moves.

We always had so much energy we had to be playing and running. That doesn't seem to be true anymore back in Houston or even in the Chicago area. You'll find some kids in the inner city shooting hoops all day, and those are the kids who will excel in high school and beyond. But you don't see those corner lots *full* of kids running and playing football and baseball.

What are all those kids doing? They start by watching television. There's always some cartoon or silly show to watch. And then as they get older, without supervision, they're watching adult shows and movies they have no business watching. Their lives are boring, so they try to fill their time with that kind of entertainment. They play video games for hours, hang out in malls, and do dope. Idle time is a dangerous thing.

Idle time is a dangerous thing.

When we lived on the North Shore of Chicago, Kim and I noticed that when we drove past the high schools, kids out on the track or in the field looked out of shape. They could hardly run. They were overweight or weak or exhausted. You can't count on a few minutes a day in a gym class to keep you in shape. You have to walk everywhere you go, do a lot of running, and play constantly. We're raising a whole generation of out-of-shape kids. It's sad.

Kids are different in many ways today, and why? When I was growing up we were expected to call men and women *sir* and *ma'am*. We were told to respect them and eventually, because we had to speak to them with respect, we did. I hear kids all the time now calling adults by their first names, saying "What?" when they don't hear something, instead of, "Pardon me?" or "Sir?" It sounds terrible. When a kid says, "Huh?" it just goes right through me. I even hear children address their relatives by their first names only, instead of using Aunt and Uncle.

Maybe it isn't so bad that we aren't as rigid and formal as we were in Texas twenty-five years ago, but today kids really *don't* respect their elders. I've been on a bus, in a waiting room, and even in a cafeteria where all the seats are taken and a couple of elderly women come in. I'm the only person to stand and offer my seat. What ever happened to manners and chivalry?

Once when I was a child I was walking home from school when I noticed a newspaper outside the fence at a house. It didn't occur to me to leave it there. I did what my dad would have done. I picked it up, opened the fence, and tossed it in. As I was closing the gate I noticed a woman standing in the doorway of the house.

She hollered something at me.

"Ma'am?"

"What'd you say, boy?"

"I said, 'Ma'am.' I didn't hear you."

"Where do you live, boy?"

"Up the street over there, ma'am."

"What church do you go to?"

"The Pentecostal, ma'am."

"Your daddy the preacher?"

"Yes, ma'am."

"You're a Singletary boy then?"

"Yes, ma'am."

"Com'ere, boy," she said. I didn't know what I had gotten myself into. She knew who I was because of the way I spoke and because of what I had done. She asked me my first name and then thanked me for being so kind about her paper. I was embarrassed. I hadn't thought it was any big deal. It was the way people were supposed to be. The paperboy should have gotten it over her fence to start with.

I remember my father talking to men half his age and calling them *sir*. It wasn't out of fear. It was common courtesy. He treated everyone with dignity and respect. Kids today aren't going to all of the sudden pick that up when they're twenty.

I still call people *sir* and *ma'am*, and it's offensive to some—especially certain women. But I'm sorry. It's the way I was raised, and it's the only way I know. I mean it respectfully, so no one should take it as too much deference or as an implication that they are older than I am.

I know there will be those who say that I'm complaining about simple changes in style and culture. But I think out-of-shape kids, disrespect for elders, bored teens with nothing better to do than hang around—all that is a symptom of a deeper problem. The problem is self-worth. Nobody cares about anybody but himself anymore.

I remember one Sunday at Baylor when a bunch of us in the athletic dorm were in the TV room relaxing for a couple of hours. Somebody saw an old couple in out-of-date clothes walking toward the door and said, "Who's that? Look at those threads!" If it had been my parents I would have popped somebody, but it wasn't. It was the parents of a basketball player sitting near me, and they must have sacrificed to get him sharp clothes because he was always dressed fine. He looked out the door and saw them coming, rolled his eyes, and headed the other way. He went out the back and called to them before they got to the door. He was that embarrassed of his own parents. I was disgusted.

Our society has turned into a true me-first mess. Take care of yourself, watch out for the competition, don't trust anyone. Do it to him before he does it to you. Nobody cares about you. If you get a chance to get ahead, take it. Once you develop that kind of a mentality, it's tough to relax and enjoy life. You

But I think out-of-shape kids, disrespect for elders, bored teens with nothing better to do than hang around—all that is a symptom of a deeper problem. The problem is self-worth. Nobody cares about anybody but himself anymore.

spend your whole life keeping up with the Joneses, and your kids are getting away from you. Each generation seems to have fewer and fewer responsible citizens who are willing to carry the torch. They're bored to death because they believe no one cares about them. And if no one cares, it must be because the kid is worthless. It's a tragedy.

It's getting to the point now where even if a kid has selfworth and applies himself to his school work, he can't go to college unless he's rich or an athlete. I believe the United Negro College Fund slogan "A mind is a terrible thing to waste." In this country, in this day and age, no kid's mind should go to waste. Why can't every kid who wants to go to college be able to go? Nobody can tell me there isn't enough money floating around to put kids through school who qualify.

We spend fifty million dollars and more to make movies. We pay some athletes five million dollars a season to play ball. We pay corporation presidents millions of dollars a year. We put billions into space and defense. Isn't there some money somewhere so that every kid who will work hard but can't afford college would be able to go? Maybe the professional sports leagues should put a little money aside out of every salary, benefit, and pension fund. Maybe some of the proceeds from television or the play-offs should go toward a scholarship program for non-athletes.

Why is it that the only poor blacks you see in major universities are scholarship athletes? Many of them apply themselves less to their studies than other students do. They take advantage of the scholarship to simply play football and wait to be drafted. Then they make enough money that they could pay back their scholarship many times over. If they did that, other kids could go to college. Somehow, some way, if industry gets involved too, there has to be a way in this country that a kid who has the grades and the desire should be able to go to college. That would go a long way in turning back some of the bad influences that are affecting the society. If it's true that not too far into the next century the people who are in the minority now will be the majority, it would seem that everyone would want underprivileged people to be prepared and educated. How many great minds are out there that we'll never know about because they never had the opportunity or were never encouraged because they weren't athletes great enough to have their educations paid for?

I'm not talking about giving things to people who think the world owes them a living. I'm talking about kids who are willing to work their tails off. When I was growing up, we didn't take handouts. I probably would not have accepted a four-year scholarship to college if I hadn't thought I earned it by my football playing and staying in shape. And I certainly wouldn't have kept it if I hadn't worked to keep my grades up, because that's how it worked at Baylor.

My parents were proud people. There were those who tried to give us stuff. Mom and Dad said if they couldn't afford it, they didn't need it or want it. If a friend tried to give us food or clothing, Mom and Dad insisted on doing something in return—washing clothes for them or fixing things around their house. Mom and Dad didn't want anything for free. I don't fault them for that. That same attitude has kept me and Kim out of debt. You don't see much of that kind of pride anymore. People always have their hands out. They begin to think they're due for a change in life-style. They think they deserve more, but they're not willing to work for it. They complain and grumble and decide, "That should be my house. That should be my car. That should be my wife." Scripture warns against coveting and calls it sin. It dominates our society.

The welfare system encourages that sin. I believe it is the country's responsibility to support the elderly and the handicapped. We have a responsibility to help those who truly aren't able to work and support themselves. I've never understood how our country can support people who are perfectly able to work. They sit at home and draw a check. They drive to other cities and claim they live there and draw checks from there too. Experts will tell you it would take millions of dollars to monitor all that and get rid of the swindlers, but it's costing us that much to live with them.

There should be strong penalties for welfare fraud, and I'm not just talking about people drawing more than one check. I'm talking about anyone drawing even one check when he could be working. Not everybody has to be a ditch digger or a construction worker. If there is a physical problem, do what you can. Learn to type. Talk on the phone. Run a computer. There are all kinds of jobs for people who are willing. I'm always challenged and encouraged when I see the mentally and physically handicapped learning a trade and staying at it day after day. It gives them a sense of responsibility and self-worth. They're contributing to society, earning their way, not sitting back and expecting a regular check for nothing. If they can do it, a good percentage of the welfare recipients can do it.

My favorite excuse for people not working is when they say there is no job out there right now for which they are not overqualified. So in other words, if the job is beneath you and your education would be wasted on it, you should just sit at home and let me pay your bills? I don't think so. Keep those resumés going out while you earn a paycheck in another field. Your day will come.

Again, my dad comes to mind. He has worked just about every day of his life, and I know there were plenty of times when he could have justified staying in bed. He had sore muscles, sprained joints, the flu, busted fingers, arthritis, you name it. He was out there working anyway. Anybody in this country who wants to work can find a job somewhere. Nobody needs to go hungry, jobless, or homeless. Times can get tough. Any ghetto child like me knows that. But I won't let circumstances or pride stand between me and a chance to work.

My best friend from Houston, Ron Williams, has always been a hard worker. He had to miss being best man in my wedding because he had started a new job and wasn't eligible for time off yet. I couldn't think of a better excuse, and I told him I completely understood. He's not the kind of guy who would lose a job and expect a handout.

Another friend of mine, Dan Rains, retired from

the Bears about five years ago. He hasn't found the "perfect" job jet. But he's always busting his tail to find work that he can do to make ends meet.

I don't know what has caused the country to fall back the way it has. It could be the school systems. When I was a kid discipline was a major thing. You just didn't get away with anything. You were there to study and learn, and you were expected to do just that. If you were there to mess around, you had to face the paddle that every teacher had. If a teacher uses a paddle today, he or she winds up in court. I know there can be abuses and you have to be careful, but we have taken authority right out of teachers' hands. The kids can say or do anything and dare the teacher to do something about it. How can kids learn in an environment like that?

If I got in trouble at school, I prayed my parents didn't find out about it, because I'd be in worse trouble at home. There was none of this going home to squeal on the teacher and then find her in trouble for something she'd done. Huh-uh.

Maybe it's better now that kids don't get in trouble for chewing gum and other small problems, but it sure seems we've gone too far when we provide smoking areas for students. Who's running the show anyway? Dress codes are out the window. I mean, it's okay for a kid to be fashionable, but when the fashion itself is sloppy—like shoelaces untied and shirttails hanging out—it's time for someone to take control again. Let somebody else have the sloppy image. There's enough of that to go around.

It all gets back to permissive child rearing, which results in troubled adults. I know men my age who spend half their day playing video games. A wife recently told me that her new husband gets up in the morning and she doesn't see him till lunch because he's playing Nintendo! He comes to bed two and three hours later than she does for the same reason. I have nothing against that game or that company, but my son and daughters are more important than any game.

It's no wonder that even adults are shallow these days. No one has anything worthwhile to say. You go to a party and by the time everybody gets done asking you about your work and commenting on the weather, the conversation is over. My wife hates it when I carry a book with me to a party, because she doesn't want me sitting off in a corner reading. But I can get real frustrated and impatient with small talk. I'm not trying to say I'm better than anyone else, but when I bring up important topics, things people should be eager to discuss, people drift away.

Raising kids is a tough job. It's scary what I see happening around me. Parents have to realize that we're raising our children for their future spouses. I just hope my kids' future spouses' parents are thinking of the same thing. Sometimes I feel I'm raising the only kids who are going to have any values when they grow up. Parents are caving in. They're letting their kids run them. They're afraid to discipline their kids because they've heard it will damage their minds, their psyches. It will turn them into rebels and all that.

We love our children very much, but the Bible says that if you raise up a child in the way he should go, he will not depart from it. Because we love our children, we discipline them. If we don't, someone else will. Maybe someone who doesn't care about the right kind of discipline.

Discipline convinces a kid he is loved and cared about. He learns that there are limits and boundaries, and that gives him a sense of security. I would never encourage discipline in anger or as only punishment. The point of discipline is correction, not revenge.

Kids sometimes need to be punished, but they should learn from it. It should never be so harsh that a child is injured, mentally or physically.

But parents aren't even disciplining their kids with rules anymore. Teens are expected to make their own decisions, and unless they are remarkably mature, they will soon be in trouble. Kids want and need rules. Josh McDowell has said that rules without relationship leads to rebellion. If that's true, then the opposite must also be true. If you have a good relationship with your child, then rules will lead to obedience.

It starts when they are small. I see kids in toy stores screaming and crying and kicking until they get what they want. I point that out to my own kids and ask them how far they think they'd get pulling something like that on Kim and me. You set the boundary before you go in the store, and you don't tolerate anything like that. If a parent is afraid to say no to his child in public, the child will soon catch on to that and get what he wants by simply making a scene. What a lesson that is for the rest of his life!

Kim and I really work hard at convincing our kids that no means no. They can ask why and they deserve an answer, but that's all. It's not open for argument. As they mature and are able to understand our reasons, more things will be open for discussion. Eventually they will be able to make their own decisions. We are trying to be good parents. We make decisions with their best interest in mind because we love them and we care about them. That is enough explaining.

My two oldest kids already coach their one-year-old sister. If we tell her no and she whines, they'll say, "Jill, that's not gonna make it."

I've seen kids at restaurants who spill things on purpose, throw food, talk loud, and make everyone uncomfortable. The parents will tell them a hundred times to stop and threaten to spank them. "I'm not going to tell you again," they say five or six times. I think a kid should be told once, and if he breaks the rule, he should be taken out and dealt with kindly in private.

Kids bug their parents when Mom or Dad are on the phone too. They have a built-in knowledge that this is an awkward situation, a time when Mommy can't control them. We nip that in the bud too. Even if we have to ask the caller to hold a minute, we will put an end to the interruption.

Mothers think that kids obey their fathers more easily just because they're afraid of them. I don't think so. I know a lot of it has to do with moms getting worn down and kids knowing how to get their own way. But I think mothers can be just as effective with kids as fathers can, if they have the energy and stamina. It's not easy, but if no means no and all instructions must be carried out, kids will do it. My son can come and jump on me and we'll play for a few minutes. If I ask him to let me work or make a call or something and he resists, he can tell from the sound of my voice that I mean it. It doesn't break his spirit or hurt our relationship. It teaches him that there is a time and a place for everything, a time to work and a time to play. Too much of either can be dangerous.

I sometimes get into trouble with relatives because of how firm I am with our kids. But I don't feel I have to defend my actions. My kids know I love them, and they also know that they have to obey, even in front of others. We don't change the rules just because we're at someone else's house or we have company. I can't worry about what other people think or how they raise their kids or would raise mine. This is my job and I will do it as unto the Lord and to the best of my ability.

You can see a big difference in society in the last twenty years in how we feel about sexual customs. When I was in high school it was hardly spoken of if an unmarried couple was living together. It was called shacking up, and it was bad. Now it's cool. The couple introduces each other as their lover or their live-in friend. How nice.

And when a girl got pregnant back then, she was shipped off someplace to have the baby, sometimes thrown out of the house or even the family, and might have had an abortion. I'm not saying those were good solutions, and of course abortion is no answer. But today we have swung so far from shame that some high schools have Baby Day when the girls with children are expected to bring them to class.

One of my teammates had a younger sister who got pregnant out of wedlock. She was encouraged to have the baby, but the family didn't show any great excitement about a grandchild on the way. In fact, she was told that she was on her own now. That sounds cold, I know, but when you make adult decisions that have adult results, you've got to grow up fast.

A relative of mine got pregnant the same way, and her parents were all excited. When is it due? What will you name it? Let's have a shower! That may seem more loving, but that girl never had to deal with the problem she had created. Now, years later, she's not married, is living with a guy, and has four kids and hardly any income. The sister of my teammate, who was made to live with her problems, has become a responsible person.

You hardly ever see tough love anymore. We don't know how to say no in love.

Well, as I said, it starts at the top. I'm afraid our

leaders are not seeking God's will as often as they used to. We've become people who care more about who's right than what's right. We should be praying for our leaders more so they'll stand for what's right.

We've become people who care more about who's right than what's right. We should be praying for our leaders more so they'll stand for what's right.

I hope I don't have to take this back while he's in office, but I think President Bush is doing a great job. To me he's one of the first presidents in a long time who has integrity. Maybe he'll wind up being the kind of president Grover Cleveland was. Cleveland ran for the Senate and then for Governor of New York, and he got both parties mad at him when he became known as the veto senator and the veto governor. He said the state was spending money it didn't have, so he just canceled all the proposed programs. The people liked his style so much he eventually became president. He did the right thing because it was the right thing, and he didn't care what the other politicians thought of him. When someone brought him evidence that his opponent had been immoral, he threw the documents in the fire and said, "Let them be the mudslingers in this campaign. That's not our style."

He was the kind of a president who took charge and took responsibility. That's the way I hope George Bush proves to have been when his term is over. Maybe it'll rub off on other leaders, and on us.

PART SIX

On Thorny Issues

16

Nobody Asked
Me, But . . .

With all my negative opin-
ions you might wonder if I have anything good to say
about America. I do. In fact, I'm extremely proud to
be an American. This is the land where dreams truly
can come true. It happened to me. This is not a perfect country by any stretch of the imagination, but
it's as close as you're going to come on this planet. No
matter where I travel around the world, there's no
place like home, especially when home is America.

I read somewhere that in Bulgaria the government

tests boys when they are eleven years old to see if they have weight lifting potential. If they do, they are moved to training centers, their families are given special privileges, and the boys are raised to be star lifters. They now dominate the sport, but I ask you: What kind of freedom is that? Most boys don't develop until they're thirteen. And what if they like another sport better? Too bad. What if their parents don't want to move and are not happy living more comfortably just because their son tested well for weight lifting potential? Too bad.

What if the kid decides at age fifteen that he doesn't like the sport anymore and he wants out? He doesn't have a choice.

There's an athlete in America who came from a communist country and has made a fortune here. When someone criticized his life-style and suggested that he was not the best role model for young people, he said that if this country was no longer open-minded, maybe he would move to the Soviet Union. Can you imagine? Someone who has come to freedom and realized a dream and made millions of dollars wanting to go back behind the iron curtain? Maybe he should go.

I don't want to be one who complains about everything without being willing to jump in with both feet and start to be part of the solution. A French social commentator once said that America is great because America is good, and that if we cease to be good, we will cease to be great. That's why I am so concerned about those areas in which we used to be good and are not anymore.

The pioneers of this country set the pace. They believed in godly ideals, and many people in America are still God-centered. When I think about that, I am grateful, and I want to pass along that history and

The pioneers of this country set the pace. They believed in godly ideals, and I want to pass along that history and that heritage to my children. It's difficult to think about, though, without wondering about what happened to some of the best things in our past.

that heritage to my children. It's difficult to think about, though, without wondering about what happened to some of the best things in our past.

Nobody asked me, but . . .

Have you ever wondered whatever happened to service in this country? When I was a kid, the local gas station was an example of service the way it should be. They checked your tires, checked your oil, washed your windows, and filled your tank. They didn't take your business for granted. They worked to make you want to come back.

When Kim and I lived on the North Shore of Chicago we liked a barbecue restaurant because the owner treated everyone like a friend. He greeted people—not just us—by name, asked about their work and their families, offered to get them extra soft drinks, and told them about his specials. There were other good barbecue places around, but we kept coming back to his. We felt special. Someone knew our name and cared about us.

After he died of cancer we went back once. The service was not the same and we have not returned.

I've been in stores where I had to ask to be waited on, and then it was by someone who didn't know much or didn't seem to care. Maybe she was filling in for someone else in a department she was unfamiliar with, but how long does it take to learn, or at least to show some sympathy to a customer? All I heard was, "I don't know. It must be back there somewhere. I saw one the other day." I'm *paying* for service like that?

I often tell my wife that if I owned a business, you would know it from the minute you walked in until the minute you walked out. People there would be trained to be service-oriented, not just because it was good for business, but also because it's the right thing to do. The clerks would be polite, they would appreciate your business, they would realize that there are other places you can go. Customers would want to come back because they would have been treated with dignity and respect and enthusiasm. And if a clerk doesn't know an answer, he or she would apologize and find someone who did.

Kim is often embarrassed with how straightforward I am with waiters or waitresses. But I don't believe in short-tipping someone if you haven't told him why. He may just think you're a cheapskate and never learn anything about service. At the end of a meal I may say, "Sir, you know what? We didn't have to come here. We chose to come here when we could have gone anywhere we wanted. You haven't smiled once. You were grumpy, and you forgot a few things. Do you think I'm going to come back here?"

Usually they don't apologize or try to make it right. They just shrug and say, "I dunno."

And I say, "Maybe your boss would like to know. I'm not saying this to make you feel bad. Hopefully the next person who comes in here will get better treatment."

I know waiting tables is thankless work and that many of the people who do it are single parents with problems at home. But we all have problems we have to leave when we're on the job. A service person's personal problems are all the more reason why he should be nice to people and serve them well enough to earn a generous tip.

I've been in places of business where I am treated shabbily until I'm recognized. Then it's, "Oh, you're Mike Singletary of the Bears! Oh, my gosh, I didn't know. Can I have your autograph?"

I have to tell you, I'm not usually too eager to oblige in a situation like that. Why should I be worth more attention and courtesy because I'm Mike Singletary than if I was just an anonymous customer? That's insulting to me, and it's sure insulting to the next guy, who may not be someone you recognize.

Nobody asked me, but . . .

Too many sportswriters write before they think. I've read columns where a guy who has never played the sport decides that a certain professional is a class D player who doesn't belong on the Bears. I believe in freedom of the press and the right of a person to express his opinion, but where does common sense and decency come in?

It's fair for a commentator to single out weaknesses and even to say where the team or an individual let down and caused a loss. But to question a person's motive or decide that he should not even have a contract, that's going too far.

Is the player allowed to defend himself? The writer will say he gets to prove himself on the field. Well, what about him and his loved ones? Are their feelings not important? There aren't too many professions in the world where someone's motives and future can be brought into question by a person outside the industry for the benefit of hundreds of thousands of readers.

How would you like someone criticizing you and deciding not only that you should be fired, but that you never should have been hired, and printing it for the whole town to read and discuss?

My motives and those of some teammates and opponents were questioned after the Bears-Giants playoff game in New York at the end of the 1990 season. I had agreed with some of the Giants before the game that when it was over we would hold hands and kneel and pray for the situation in the Persian Gulf. It was not for the press or the fans. It was just for us and for the Lord and that situation.

I had a problem to start with, because when I agreed to do it, I assumed—as I always do before a game—that we were going to win. Then, I didn't know that one of the guys I was going to kneel and hold hands with would have given me a cheap shot near the end of the game. It took real discipline to put the loss and that cheap shot behind me long enough to do what was right. We were disappointed to see the press hovering around while we prayed, but we didn't expect to be blasted in the sports pages the next day.

Commentators said we were showy, wearing our religion on our sleeves, presumptuous, intrusive. None of us were asked what we had been praying about. But if we'd been in a brawl, you can bet we would have been widely quoted. The writers don't

Commentators said we were showy, wearing our religion on our sleeves, presumptuous, intrusive. None of us were asked what we had been praying about.

want to write about the good things. Certain organizations recognize hospital visits and other charitable efforts. We're not doing that stuff for publicity, but letting the fans know about some of it might offset all the bad press players get for causing trouble, getting drunk, or driving recklessly.

Of course, players who get in trouble should not be protected from publicity. But the majority of NFL players—and most pro athletes, I think—are upstanding guys with good qualities. What about all the charity work? The jail ministries? The feeding of the hungry? The widespread social work done by so many athletes? I guess that doesn't make good journalism.

Nobody asked me, but . . .

Too many kids coming into the NFL are already in debt when they arrive. That's the fault of unscrupulous agents, and it's a tragedy. I know most agents are good and reputable, but there are just enough of the other kind that players need to beware. Worst-case scenarios go like this: An agent tells a kid he's a sure bet first or second rounder. He tells the player what that means in terms of money. Then he lends the guy the money so he can buy a fancy car or put a down payment on an expensive home.

When the kid goes in the fourth or fifth round, his first check usually goes to the agent to start paying back the loan, which was too big for a kid at that level. Then, if the player doesn't make the team, he's out of work, out of money, and in debt to the guy who was supposed to protect him from just that.

I was wined and dined by agents who promised me everything from cars to endorsements to women. It happens all the time. I was in a hotel for one of the all-American team functions when I was a senior, and I got an invitation to the room of an agent who represented a big name player in the NFL. I was suspicious right away because I knew right off that I would be second priority to the star. When I got to the room he had a beautiful blond there in an almost transparent outfit, and she smiled at me the whole time. The implication was clear. I got out of there.

The more money there is in pro football, the more agents will come out of the woodwork. Young players need to take extreme care and consult with a lot of people before signing with someone. Any time an agent tries to buy you with promises, drugs, women, or whatever—instead of advice and services—he's poison. The ones who use other guys to try to sell you, maybe big name players you respect, are also suspect.

It's impressive to a kid to think he's going to be represented by the same guy who represents a superstar. He may even get to meet the famous player. That doesn't mean a thing unless you're good enough to be drafted high and get good counsel. My advice to young players is to represent yourself if at all possible. If you feel totally over your head, then get someone you know and trust.

Nobody asked me, but . . .

Movies are going downhill. Maybe I'm becoming a prude, but I like movies without all the explicit sex and the foul language. Do these movies really represent what our society is like, or are they the reason our society is the way it is? Either way, it's a sad story.

Up until a couple of years ago I didn't even think much about it. I had not been convicted in my heart about the kinds of things I was watching. I figured it was life; that justified it. But my mother-in-law was a good example to me. She didn't want to put unclean things before her eyes. She didn't want to fill her mind with filth and bad language. So if she was over and we were watching a video or a movie that offended her, she quietly left the room.

At first that bothered me. I wondered what her problem was. I even asked Kim, "Why would she do that? That's ridiculous. Goodness, this is just life. I don't see what the big deal is about someone taking the Lord's name in vain."

A year later, when I was getting closer to the Lord, he began to convict me about what I was watching. Movies with language, nudity, and sexuality just for the lust value started to turn me off. I began to feel guilty about seeing movies like that, wondering if the Lord would be happy sitting with me there. I decided to be sure I knew what was in a movie before I watched it. So much of the stuff they put in is unnecessary and the stories would be just as good without it.

I wish someone would start selling family versions of the good movies, maybe like the ones they use on airplanes, where they take out the bad language and the nudity. You don't even miss it, and you're not offended or embarrassed. I'll bet there would be great demand for something like that. If somebody tries it, send me a commission!

Kids think they're not affected by stuff like that, but they are. What the eyes see and the ears hear is recorded in the brain. It's there and it will come out at the worst time. The Bible says that we are supposed to think on things that are pure and righteous. That doesn't include a lot of the material Hollywood has to offer.

Nobody asked me, but . . .

I'm not one who thinks pornography should be protected by the First Amendment. I know there are people who say if we censor porn, someday someone may censor the Bible, but I don't see the connection. There's nothing redeemable about pornography. When I was very young one of my brothers used to stash dirty magazines in the garage. I don't call them art. They were dirt. They were a counterfeit of God's idea, which is good, wholesome sex within marriage.

But as a kid I was curious. I would lift weights and then look at the magazines, thinking I was really learning something. At twelve, one of my brothers took me to my first peep show. I lost my father through divorce, my oldest brother to death, and my innocence at that show. It was not something I would have chosen, and I regret to this day that I got roped into it. I wish I had never put into my mind beautiful women who looked cheap. I can see how people get addicted to pornography and how bad things come of it.

Young men who get hooked on porn often see it become a monster in their lives. Serial killers and rapists often blame pornography for their start. I wish my past had been free of pornography, and I wish it wasn't so readily available today. Young people hardly have a chance of avoiding it anymore.

Nobody asked me, but . . .

There's a problem with our churches in this country. Too many of them have become country clubs, and too many others are judgmental. If you don't dress a certain way or have a certain level of income or drive a certain car, you're not really accepted.

I grew up in a church where people were publicly called down for being out of step with the way someone thought the congregation should be. That was bad enough. But now, some churches have swung so far the other way that the Word of God has been tailored to fit the congregation. The pastor is afraid to preach the meat of the Word for fear of losing members and dollars. He worries about his money coming from people rather than from God.

Rather than preaching the pure message of God, we want to be inoffensive. Jesus himself knew that the cross will divide. People don't want to hear that they are sinners in need of a Savior. It's too old-fashioned. It's too negative. It's too true.

Churches and pastors need to get back to the conviction part of the message. We need to preach the truth in love. We shouldn't condemn people but let the Word and the Spirit convict and draw them to Jesus Christ. There's a fine line between preaching only the love of God and not his judgment, but the pastor and the body of believers who truly seek the Lord will be led to just the right approach.

Nobody asked me, but . . .

Drugs are death. The drug problem in the ghetto is at least understandable, even though it needs to be fought with every weapon we have available. Kids are desperate, frustrated. They see no way out and no one is telling them how to stay straight, stay in school, and do the right thing. Those who try hardly have a chance, because the schools are bad and the system is failing. When you hear of those kids trying to escape through drugs, you can at least understand the temptation.

But what explains multi-million-dollar athletes at the top of their games resorting to drugs? Why would a guy who seemingly has everything risk it all for a temporary high that could become addictive and ruin his life?

The answer is simpler than most people realize. The important word in the above paragraph is *seemingly*. The player who has money and fame and women and attention does not have everything. He looks cool and he looks happy, but in most cases, he's not. His lifelong dream has arrived. He has reached the top and has everything this life has to give. Now what is he going to do? All that stuff still doesn't satisfy, and it never will. That peer pressure is still there from his friends. Try this, try that, you're invincible, nothing can hurt you.

Those stars are looking for escape and freedom and fulfillment where they'll never find it. That longing in their hearts is for God, not for anything this world has to offer.

Nobody asked me, but . . .

I have a little different view of homosexuality than you might think. Most straight male athletes find the idea of homosexuality repulsive. They don't tolerate it, make jokes about it, and generally despise gays.

I don't find it funny. I admit I find it repulsive, and I think that's because the Bible is clear that it is sin. But I don't despise people who are caught up in it. The blatant ones, the ones who claim God made them that way, yes, I have a problem with them. But I don't hate them. They need God.

I pity homosexuals who have not chosen the lifestyle but feel trapped in it. There is hardly a church anywhere that would help them without condemning them. I believe that Jesus would hate the sin and love the sinner, so that's what we should do too.

Tolerate it? No. Agree that God might have created some people gay? No. But love them. Pray for them. My heart goes out to people dying from AIDS. I know many of them got the disease through homosexuality, and it would be easy to say, "Well, I'm not sympathetic because they got what they deserved." All I can say is I'm glad God didn't give me what I deserved, because I deserve death too.

I believe homosexuals have to deal with their sin, but somehow we have to find a way to minister to them in love. We don't understand them and we don't seem to want to try. I associate with a lot of men who would just as soon spit on a homosexual as to pray for him. God's example is different. God loves him in spite of his sin and wants him to be free.

Nobody asked me, but . . .

I believe premarital and extramarital sex are wrong. Young people should be urged to stay pure and given practical advice on how to do just that. The best birth control and precaution against disease is abstinence, and it's as old as the Bible itself. What a wonderful gift one's virginity is to his spouse! There's a place for wild, wonderful, abandoned, passionate, sexual love. It's the marriage bed. It was God's idea, and he does everything right.

I wish someone had sat me down in high school and given me all the reasons to stay pure. I wish I had had better examples than many of the men I looked up to, who played church on Sunday and had women outside their marriages during the week. Illicit sex was almost expected in my community, but it was still wrong.

Nobody asked me, but . . .

Abortion is murder. If that unborn baby is not a human being, I don't know what it is. Don't think I have a knee-jerk reaction to such a touchy issue. I haven't always felt this way. I say to my shame that if a friend had asked me for money for an abortion when I was in college—even if it wasn't my responsibility at all—I would have provided it.

I have since come to believe that the unborn baby is the innocent party in rape, incest, and unwanted pregnancies of any type. If someone is to be put to death, it should be the perpetrator of the crime, not one of the innocent parties.

I'm not insensitive to the terrible problems caused by childhood pregnancies, and I don't pretend to be a medical or psychological expert. But it's shortsighted to think anything is solved by adding abortion to the trauma of an unwanted pregnancy.

I totally disagree with Christians who fight abortion by violence. That doesn't make sense to me, though I can understand their frustration. They would say that violence is acceptable when you're trying to prevent a homicide, and that's hard to argue with. But young women heading into an abortion clinic need love and counseling, not more confusion. They need to know that their bodies are not their own. They were bought with a price.

Nobody asked me, but . . .

I've tried to solve every modern problem facing mankind. How'd I do? I'm sorry if some of my answers to major problems sound simplistic. If you sat with me and we could talk for a few hours, you'd know that I have thought and prayed and sought answers from Scripture. You and I may not agree on everything, but at least we know that these are important topics that should be discussed by thinking people.

You can see why small talk bores me and makes me impatient. Issues of life and death can be decided upon only by people who are willing to do their homework and develop their insights and opinions through seeking God's wisdom.

Issues of life and death can be decided upon only by people who are willing to do their homework and develop their insights and opinions through seeking God's wisdom.

I know life is full of happiness and smiles and good surprises too. We can't dwell on the down side of everything all the time. But don't be afraid to tackle the thorny issues occasionally. The conclusions you come to and the way you present them to others may have more impact on their lives than anything else you ever talk about.

17

On Being a Christian Without Being Religious

I get a lot of invitations to speak at functions celebrating black achievements, which I enjoy doing. But I'm not sure they're always celebrating the right black achievements. I take fewer and fewer invitations to speak at functions like that.

I think many of us have forgotten what's really important in life. It's not only the well-known musician who has important things to say. Or the well-paid athlete who changes the course of history. It's okay to be a musician or athlete if that's your gift. But some of us have other talents. Just because you're not a musician or athlete doesn't mean life is over. You can still do something important.

George Washington Carver, Booker T. Washington, Crispus Attus, and Martin Luther King, Jr., realized that they could make a difference in spite of everything they had against them. They showed leadership, character, integrity. They touched the world and gave hope that never existed before. If it could be done then, it could certainly be done now. There are a few people—such as General Colin Powell and Andrew Young—who continue that tradition. But too many have dropped the torch.

Satan has locked many young blacks into self-pity and despair. They don't see a way out, except the occasional basketball or football scholarship. Young guys and girls think, "I couldn't own my own company. I don't even have the money to go to college," or "I couldn't become a surgeon or a lawyer; the whole system is against me. Why try?"

But God can free us. When he does, we are no longer limited by our fears and cultural perceptions. We can make an impact on others in spite of what goes on around us. He gives us the courage to be all he has gifted us to be.

I recently wrote a poem that summarizes my thoughts on the issues facing the black community. I call it "Black Man."

> Black man, black man, can't you see? It's on the news, it's on TV.
> The enemy is coming, the enemy is here.
> Why can't we understand we have a higher call than singing songs and playing ball.
>
> Black man, black man, please look again. The real enemy is not white skin.

But it just may be your so-called friend,
Who tells you what you can and cannot do—how life is so hard on me and you.

Break away, free yourself, get advice from someone else.
This message is not for those of thin skin. Know the facts if your intent is to win.
Know the truth and what it means, starting with John three-sixteen.

The master of deception is like a great wind, blowing through the inner city, killing its men.
Abortion, AIDS, gangs, cocaine, crack just to name a few, drive-by shootings kill the innocent too.
When will it stop, when will it end—this treacherous thing God calls sin?

Come, come nearer, look in the mirror. Did all those great men before us die in vain?
Men like Lincoln, Martin Luther King; they stood for freedom and equal rights.
What took them years to gain can be lost overnight.

As you look staring at this mirror, are things becoming a little clearer?
We need more men, men who will remain pure:
God-fearing men who are afraid of only God Himself.
Men who are obedient to God's Word.
Men who will speak the truth in love.
Men who will seek God's wisdom and forsake their own.
Men who will pray for one another, love one another, encourage one another.
Men who will raise their children.
Men who will stay one-woman men.

If we do this, Satan will have to flee.
It starts with you, it starts with me.
It started with Jesus at Calvary.

Being a Christian athlete is a very uncool thing to be, unless you are religious. Being religious is cool. You can even be popular. You're known as a pretty straight guy who mentions God a lot and you can still live fairly up-to-date. Religion is an attempt to bring Christianity into the twentieth century. When I was religious I picked and chose those things in the Bible I could live with, and I explained away the rest. My logic, or lack of it, went something like: "Surely God doesn't expect us to follow *this* teaching in *this* day and age!"

When I was a religious guy, I was a great, great compromiser. I knew how to pick the people I compared myself to. I always chose the guys who fell by the wayside and made me look good. I certainly didn't pick the guys who were walking what they were talking. I chose the ones who were just talking. And that is religion. Religious guys want to be seen as good people. They are judgmental and know who's got real problems. Their own are hidden and not talked about.

The true Christian, however, the true believer, is not concerned about what he looks like in society. He is less concerned with hurting feelings if he's speaking the truth in love. The true Christian measures himself by Christ and knows that he always falls short of that standard. Yet he prays and studies and works toward imitating Christ, being one of his. The true believer knows that all glory for all achievements is due Jesus and not himself. He knows that the only thing that separates him from anyone else is grace. The believer is just as much in need of a Savior as anyone else, and he knows that nothing he could ever do would make him worthy of what Christ has done for him.

I love to do charity work, but I constantly fight the

The true Christian is not concerned about what he looks like in society. He measures himself by Christ and knows that he always falls short of that standard.

battle with pride. Why am I doing this? Is it just to be seen of men? Do I want people to say that Singletary is always doing nice things, that he remembers where he came from, that he loves children? If I'm doing it for any reason other than true compassion and as unto the Lord, I shouldn't be doing it.

The person who is a true believer—a follow of Christ, a Christian, and not simply religious—is one who also knows that there is an evil one. It is not fashionable today to believe in a personal devil, Satan. People make fun of that. Flip Wilson had a running gag about doing something wrong ("The devil made me do it!"). And even the Church Lady on "Saturday Night Live" blames sin on the devil ("Who could it be? Oh, I don't know. Maybe, SATAN!?").

But Satan is no joke. He's real and he's at work, and most people don't even know it. They don't believe he exists, so they aren't even aware of what he does in their lives. Satan is the great counterfeiter. He takes something that God made perfect, then he twists it so it still looks attractive while it kills you. The Bible is clear that he is a thief who is out to steal, kill, and destroy. He attacks believers, and he attacks marriages, and he attacks churches. Pornography, premarital and extramarital sex, and homosexuality are counterfeits of the sexual love within marriage, which was God's idea. Materialism, looking out for number one, and egotism are counterfeits of God's idea of achieving by serving others.

Christians need to know who their enemy is before they can wage war against him. Too many of us find a discussion of Satan so repulsive that we just shut him out of our minds. I know there is danger in giving him too much credit, but we should at least know that he is the great deceiver. For years I was a defeated man because I was trying to resist temptation with small artillery. Satan was throwing the real fiery darts, and I was losing. I could lie as easily as I told the truth. I was fearful, afraid of the dark, afraid of the future, afraid of life.

I could get up in public and talk about God as if I knew him, but I really didn't. I was always looking over my shoulder to see if there was someone there who knew the real me and could call me a liar for pretending that I was a man of God. Everything I did was for my own benefit. I looked out for Mike. If it wasn't good for me, I didn't do it. I was talking a God walk, but I wasn't walking what I was talking. I could get up and speak for God, but I was as empty as I could be. You've seen the graffiti about sleeping with the light on? That was me. I went to sleep with a light or the TV on every night. When I was single and we had a Thursday game, I might go to my place

I was always looking over my shoulder to see if there was someone there who knew the real me and could call me a liar

and leave the lights or TV or music on until the next Monday. I was afraid of the dark. I knew something was wrong.

That life is a long way from where I needed to be. I wanted to get to the point where I could talk to God like a friend, where I was not being defeated by Satan at every turn. It feels so good to be able to speak plainly with God and say, "Lord I'm having a tough time here. I need your wisdom, your strength, your mercy. I need you."

It was only when God began to deal with the sin in my life and I reconciled with my father and confessed to my wife that I began to experience what it meant to have Christ in my heart. I'm not saying that it was anything that I did that made me a Christian. God gave me the strength to do what needed to be done, once I had put my full trust in him.

Too many guys are interested in true Christianity, but they run the other way when they think about what it would mean to their private lives. They have no interest in sexual purity or cleaning up their language or changing any of their ways. I try to tell them, God takes you as you are and he'll do whatever changing needs to be done.

When Kim and I got married, other couples would tell us they envied us because I was such a man of God and had been so true to her during our engagement period. That went right through me. I thought getting married would make me what I knew God wanted me to be, but it's never automatic. God had work to do in my heart.

I encourage Christians to grow. Going to church a couple of times a week, getting into a Bible study, reading the Bible a little bit each day, that's not going to do it. You have to get serious, get systematic. Develop an inner life of prayer and really get into the Word every day. Buy some commentaries and Bible study books and discover what God has to say to you. If you don't, Satan will get a deceitful little foothold in your life. He'll tell you that you're doing plenty. You're not a big sinner, and you're often seen in church. You are not growing and you're not effective, but you're getting by, and who can ask for more than that? See how subtle he can be? He's a great strategist, and we need real ammunition to defeat him.

Satan wants us to look at our circumstances and to make our decisions based on logic and what other people think, not based on the Word of God, which never changes. The true believer will walk by faith, not by sight. But it takes dedication and persistence in the Word.

What a joy it is to live in the knowledge that the power that raised Jesus from the dead is available to us! When Jesus defeated death and rose again, he defeated any scheme Satan can come up with. Satan was defeated that day, and all we have to do is to live in that knowledge and confidence. The Bible says we can defeat Satan by resisting him, and he will flee. I believe the Scripture that says, "He who is in you is greater than he who is in the world" (1 John 4:4b). The he that is in you is Jesus, and the he that is in the world is Satan. We win!

I resist Satan by quoting Scripture (like the above) to him when I feel he's trying to defeat me. Sometimes I just pray, "Lord, he's trying to do it again. Help me to resist him."

Kim's grandmother and her aunt were stopped at a light in Detroit once when a man opened their car door and grabbed their purses. He tried to pull the rings off Kim's grandmother's fingers, so she just spoke aloud, "Jesus. Jesus. In the name of Jesus I command you to leave us alone."

The man screamed, "Shut up! Shut up! Shut up!" But she just kept using the name of Jesus. Every time he touched her hand he jerked away as if he'd been shocked. "What have you got in there?" he demanded.

"Jesus," she repeated softly. And he ran off.

People are bound and unable to use God's power against Satan, because Satan is such an accuser. For years, every time I wanted to take a step of faith, Satan would tell me, "Man, God's not going to hear your prayer. Remember all the things you've done." Satan can play the tapes of anyone's sin, running it through their mind at just the right time to keep them defeated. But we don't have to be any better or cleaner when we turn to God for strength and forgiveness than we did when we were lost and dead in our sins and turned to him for salvation. He's still the same God. He still takes us as we are. Then he will give us the strength to be what he wants us to be.

When I first joined the Bears and was only religious, not truly living the life of a Christian, I was judgmental. I decided that players who smoked or drank or swore could not be Christians. I set myself up in my own mind as better than they were, and I justified being a phony. I know now that it is God who takes care of the inconsistencies, and that it is the heart that determines where a man stands with God.

Since God has established himself in my life, I have grown to the point where sometimes he can use me to counsel players. Many come to me with problems, and a lot of them want to tell me about things they're caught up in and feel bad about. They're always shocked to hear that I have been through many of the same things.

There was a time, however, when God impressed deep upon my heart that he wanted me to confront another Christian on the team who was clearly straying from him. I resisted that like everything. I didn't want that kind of a confrontation. But God's Spirit would not let up on me. I felt it in my heart every day to say something. This man was not being faithful to his wife, and I knew he had to be miserable.

On a team bus to the airport after a game I sat next to him. We bantered back and forth about nothing for a while, then I looked seriously at him. It was as if he knew what was coming. "I don't want to talk to you about this," I said. "You have to believe it's a message from someone else, and you know who I'm talking about." He turned away from me and looked out the window in the darkness. I kept talking. "I hope you listen, because I'm just the messenger. Whatever is going on in your life, you should think twice about it. Think of your wife. Think of your kids. Don't let them down. They need you. This could cost you everything."

He didn't say anything for a long time, but he wiped away tears. "It's difficult, Mike," he whispered. "So difficult. I'm going through a lot."

"I know that," I said. "All we can do is pray. Let's pray right now." And we did. He seems to be doing better now. He's still with his wife. I have not felt led of God to be his watchdog. I was led to talk to him and pray with him. It's a wonderful thing to be used of God.

Kim and I have felt fortunate to be able to help out with the raising of one of my nieces. What happened was that my mother had to raise many of my nieces and nephews, and one of the last nieces is a high schooler named Rumonda. I remember when she was a little girl and she would sit and talk with me at the kitchen table when I came home from high school. I tried to help teach her manners, how to answer the phone and the door, how to talk to people, strangers to avoid, that type of thing. I lost the chance to have much impact on her when I left home, and meanwhile, she was growing up.

She began having trouble in school, and my mother needed help with her. Mom isn't getting any younger, and handling a teenager is a lot to take at this stage of her life. Rumonda seemed to lack self-worth and drive and was hanging around with the wrong crowd. When Kim and I saw her in Houston she didn't say much, seemed shy and not socially minded. She felt restricted by her grandmother and was frustrated. I was worried about her.

I saw that she needed to get out of Houston, but I didn't want to suggest it to Kim. We had our own home and our own kids, and it would be asking a lot of a wife to bring in a frustrated teenager. I prayed and told the Lord that I cared about Rumonda, that I saw tremendous potential and a girl who needed to know she was loved by being offered a better chance in life. I thought she was a great girl and I didn't want to see her give up on life. But I said nothing to Kim.

Before we left Houston, Kim came to me. "Mike," she said, "I understand what Rumonda is going through. Why don't we think about bringing her up to live with us for a while."

I was stunned. "Kim, you'd better think this through. This is a teenager. This is going to be work, more work than we think. I love you for thinking of it. Let's pray about it."

We prayed and thought about it for a couple of days and decided to do it, with God's help. My mother and Rumonda were thrilled. We got all the guardianship paperwork started and Kim worked with the local high school to get credits transferred. Then Rumonda moved in with us.

We told her right from the beginning what we expected. She would go to school every day. She would be expected to study and to do her best. No skipping school. No cutting classes. She would have chores. She would have a curfew. She would also have some freedom. We told her we expected her to hold her head up when she spoke to people, to look them in the eye, to be polite. I told her to never refer to herself as less than anyone else and that we don't use the words *can't* and *won't* in our house. "In this family we love the Lord, we love each other, and we love you. Treat this place as your house and these kids as your brothers and sisters. Treat us like we treat you. If you see something that needs picking up, pick it up. Something that needs doing, do it."

We got her into the practice of eating breakfast, drinking milk, juice, and water, getting healthy. No more popcorn or potato chips first thing in the morning. We talked with her about life, plans, goals, ambitions, dreams. Her schoolwork immediately improved. Her color was better, her smile was radiant. She was gaining confidence. Her grades shot up and she began thinking about college.

She'd been here a month when she asked if she could take our brand-new Suburban out for a drive. She had a learner's permit and wanted to practice. I said sure. A few minutes later Kim came in with the news. Rumonda had not made it out of the gate before scraping the new car. She was crying when I got out there. "Lord," I prayed silently, "give me wisdom here."

It came immediately. I thought of a receiver who has dropped a pass. What does the team do? Throw to him again immediately.

"Rumonda," I said, "I want you to get back in the truck and try it again. Use your mirrors, be careful, do it right."

Remember this day and pass along a little of God's grace that has been passed on to you.

I had her drive in and out of the driveway ten or fifteen times. She looked shocked that I wasn't mad. When she was finished I got her out of the truck and showed her the damage. "This can be fixed," I said. "But it will all be a waste if you didn't learn anything. You have to use your mirrors. You have to be aware of everything. Now stop crying. I'm not mad at you. I want you to remember this day when some snotty-nosed teenager asks to use your new car and makes a mistake. Don't yell at the kid. Remember this day and pass along a little of God's grace that has been passed on to you."

She's going to be fine. She's got a lot to learn, and it won't be easy. We're trying to change habits that have taken a lifetime to form. I think Rumonda can see that we set guidelines and stick to them because we love her and have her best interest at heart. She may chafe under some of them now, but we believe she will see the value of them someday. We love having her with us and, even though it is a lot of work, we consider it a privilege from God.

Life in Christ is meaningless without the opportunities he sends our way to flesh it out, to live it the way he expects. I think of that when I wonder what the future holds. I don't know how much longer I'll be a player/coach or what I'll be doing with my life a few years from now. But I know I will continue to seek God's will and try to do what he wants. Whether I'm in the ministry or in business, coaching, broadcasting, or running a sports medicine facility, I'll be striving to share his good news with people.

I'll still be an old-fashioned, conservative, do-the-best-I-can kind of a guy, and I'll still be married to the most wonderful wife in the world. She'll be trying to get me to smile more, lighten up some, and not take life so seriously. I'll be doing the best I can to make her happy as we both work at serving the Lord.

CAREER STATISTICS

MIKE SINGLETARY   **50**
Linebacker   **Baylor**   **11th year**
Ht: 6-0   **Wt: 228**

Born: 10/9/58 Houston, Texas
Acquistion: Second round (38th player) of 1981 draft.

PRO CAREER: Winner of 1990 NFL Man of the Year for playing excellence and off-the-field contributions . . . Defensive captain since 1983 . . . Finished as team's first or second leading tackler each of last nine seasons . . . His 140 starts, 1,229 tackles, 767 solo stops, 47 passes defended, and 13 fumble recoveries are most on current team . . . Missed just two games in career . . . Named to NFL Team of the '80s by Pro Football Hall of Fame Board of Selectors . . . Pro Bowl after 1983, '84, '85, '86, '87, '88, '89, and '90 seasons.

1990 SEASON: All-NFC first-team by UPI and Pro Football Weekly . . . Led team in tackles (151) for fifth time in his career and third straight year . . . Set career-high with 20 tackles, 10 solo, in being named NFC Defensive Player of the Week for game at Denver (11/18) . . . Had 17 tackles (eight solo) at Raiders (9/30) . . . Game ball effort with eight tackles vs. Rams (10/14) . . . Registered 11 stops at Minnesota (11/25) and two weeks later at Washington . . . Nine tackles (four solo), two passes defended, and six-yard sack at Phoenix (10/28). Games played-started: 16-16

PREVIOUS SEASONS: 1989 — Named to seventh straight Pro Bowl; all-NFL by The Sporting News and AP; all-NFC by UPI and Pro Football Weekly . . . Turned in seven 10-plus-tackle games; totalled 151 on the year . . . Game ball for season-high 14 tackles, eight solo, pass defended, and fumble caused on Monday night vs. Eagles in Week 4 . . . Along with McMichael, was only defensive player to start all 16 games . . . Missed second-half of season finale at San Francisco (12/24) with bruised ribs . . . Grabbed only interception vs. Tampa Bay (11/19) . . . 13 tackles, seven solo at Tampa Bay (10/8); 12 stops vs. Houston (10/15) and vs. Tampa Bay. **1988 —** Capped off brilliant season by earning sixth consecutive trip to Pro Bowl as one of just two unanimous selections (Reggie White) . . . Named NFL Defensive Player of the Year by AP and Pro Football Weekly; NFC Defensive Player of Year by UPI and Football News . . . First-team all-NFL by AP, PFWA, TSN and PFW; first-team all-NFC by UPI and Football News . . . Led club with a career-high 170 tackles, including 89 solo, also a team best . . . Established new single game career-high with 16 tackles vs. Cowboys (10/16) and at Tampa Bay (11/20) . . . Intercepted pass and recovered fumble at Tampa Bay . . . Other top games: 16 tackles vs. Tampa Bay (11/8) and 14 at New England (10/30) . . . Had 10+ tackles in eight games. **1987 —** Named to virtually every all-pro team . . . Second on team in tackles (108), solo (55), and forced fumbles (three) . . . Had 14 tackles at Tampa Bay (10/26) . . . Had three other double-digit tackle performances and twice had nine stops . . . Both sacks came in season-opening 34–19 win over Giants (9/14) . . . Injured finger at Minnesota (12/6) required 12 stitches during game; returned to lead goal-line stand in division-clinching 30–24 win. **1986** — Unanimous all-pro selection . . . Had 79 tackles in first seven games before pulling groin at Minnesota (10/19) causing him to break streak of 73 starts . . . Had 14 tackles vs. Eagles (9/14) and 13 stops vs. Minnesota (10/5). **1985** — NFL Defensive Player of the Year by AP; NFC Defensive Player of the Year by UPI . . . Consensus all-NFL choice after 113 tackles . . . NFC Defensive Player of Week vs. Patriots (9/15) after seven tackles, three sacks and interception . . . Had 13 tackles and sack in playoffs; two fumble recoveries in Super Bowl XX. **1984** — Leading tackler with 116 . . . Consensus all-NFL . . . Second with three forced fumbles. 1983 — Teams leading tackler with 148 while being named a consensus all-NFL choice . . . Led team with four fumble recoveries. **1982** — Tied for second on club with 71 tackles. **1981** — Started last nine games earning all-rookie honors by PFWA, UPI, PFW and Football Digest . . . Earned first game ball following 10-tackles and forced fumble effort vs. Kansas City (11/8) . . . Bears received choice to draft him by swapping second round picks with 49ers (to skip past Vikes) and giving San Francisco additional fifth round selection.

COLLEGIATE, PERSONAL: One of greatest players in conference history . . . Earned consensus all-American honors final two seasons while being dubbed SWC Player of Year both years . . . Only junior selected to all-SWC Team of the '70s . . . Averaged 15 tackles per game over career at Baylor . . . Established school record with 232 tackles in '78 . . . Posted 20+tackles in four games; 30+ tackles 3 times including career-high 33 stops vs. Arkansas . . . Never had fewer than 10 tackles in game . . . Finalist in '80 Lombardi Trophy voting . . . Served as team captain final two seasons . . . Final college stats: 662 tackles, 351 solos, 18 passes defended, six fumble recoveries . . . Attended Houston's Warthing High . . . Active in community services speaking to various youth groups in Chicago and Houston; FCA, Hemophilia Foundation of Illinois, Drug and Substance Abuse . . . Favorite book: *The Amazing Results of Positive Thinking* by Norman Vincent Peale . . . Co-authored book, *Calling the Shots,* after 1985 season . . . BA degree in management . . . Aspires to own health spa/resort . . . Nickname: Samurai . . . Uncle of Tampa Bay LB Broderick Thomas . . . Given name Michael Singletary . . . Married (Kim) . . . Daughters (Kristen, Jill) and son (Matthew) . . . Resides in Chicago, IL.

Singletary's Pro Stats

	Interceptions				Tkls/	Force	Fum	Pass	Sack-	
	No	Yds	Lg	TD	Solo	Fum	Rec	Def	Yds	G-GP
1990	0	0	0	0	151-67	0	2	4	1-6	16-16
1989	0	0	0	0	151-79	2	0	5	1-2	16-16
1988	1	13	13	0	170-89	0	1	3	1-3	16-16
1987	0	0	0	0	108-55	3	1	4	2-14	16-12
1986	1	3	3	0	129-68	1	0	3	2-15	14-14
1985	1	23	23	0	113-89	0	3	5	3-24	16-16
1984	1	4	4	0	116-81	3	1	4	3.5-24	16-16
1983	1	0	0	0	148-118	1	4	7	3.5-23.5	16-16
1982	0	0	0	0	71-61	1	1	2	1-9	9-9
1981	1	−3	−3	0	72-60	1	0	4	0-0	16-9
Career	6	40	23	0	1,229-767	12	13	47	18-120.5	147-140
Play-offs										
1990	0	0	0	0	15-5	0	0	0	0-0	2-2
1988	0	0	0	0	13-4	0	0	1	0-0	2-2
1987	0	0	0	0	7-0	0	0	0	0-0	1-1
1986	0	0	0	0	12-7	0	0	0	0-0	1-1
1985	0	0	0	0	15-10	3	0	2	1-11	3-3
1984	0	0	0	0	9-4	0	0	2	0-0	2-2
Career	0	0	0	0	71-32	3	0	5	1-11	11-11

Singletary's Single Game Highs

Tackles: 20 at Den* (11/18/90)   Sacks: 3 vs. NE (9/15/85)
Solos: 14 at GB (11/3/85)
*Overtime game

BEARS MIDDLE LINEBACKERS

Hall of Famer Bill George (1952–65) is given credit for creating the middle linebacker by dropping off the line of scrimmage from his "middle guard" position. He was succeeded by another Hall of Famer, Dick Butkus, who roamed the middle for nine seasons (1965–73). Three players —Don Rives (1973–75), Larry Ely (1976), and Tom Hicks (1976–80)— took turns at the spot until Mike Singletary claimed the job in 1981 and has held it ever since.

ABOUT THE AUTHORS

Mike Singletary grew up in Houston, Texas, the youngest of ten children. He attended Baylor University, where he earned a bachelor's degree in business administration. He has played middle linebacker for the Chicago Bears for ten years and is the only player/coach in the NFL. He has written his autobiography, *Calling the Shots*.

Singletary lives in Chicago, Illinois, with his wife, Kim, and their children: Kristen, Matthew, and Jill.

Jerry Jenkins is a widely published author of biographies and fiction. He has written the biographies of Orel Hershiser (on the *New York Times* Bestseller List for nine weeks), Joe Gibbs, Meadowlark Lemon, Hank Aaron, Walter Payton, B.J. Thomas, Dick Motta, and Luis Palau.

Jenkins is writer-in-residence at Moody Bible Institute. Born in Kalamazoo, Michigan, he lives outside Zion, Illinois, with his wife, Dianna, and their three sons: Dallas, Chad, and Michael.